SHAKESPEARE AND BURBAGE

Shakespeare and Burbage

The sound of Shakespeare as devised to suit
the voice and talents of his principal player

by

MARTIN HOLMES

with an introduction by
J. C. Trewin

PHILLIMORE

1978

Published by
PHILLIMORE & CO., LTD.,
London and Chichester
Head Office: Shopwyke Hall, Chichester,
Sussex, England

ISBN 0 85033 306 7

Printed in England by
UNWIN BROTHERS, LTD.,
at the Gresham Press, Old Woking, Surrey

and bound at
THE NEWDIGATE PRESS, LTD.,
at Book House, Dorking, Surrey

To
Helen

CONTENTS

LIST OF PLATES
(between pages 84 and 85)

I   Self-portrait of Richard Burbage, in Dulwich College Picture Gallery

II   A Franciscan at Prayer, by Francisco Zurbaran (1598-1662)

III   Richard Tarlton, the famous Elizabethan clown, from whom Armin learnt his art. From an elaborate initial in the British Library MS Harl. 3885

IV   King Henry VIII towards the end of his life. Contemporary copy of a portrait by Holbein

LIST OF FIGURES

INTRODUCTION

Many years ago, when my housemaster was asking his boys what they had done during the vacation, one of them said hopefully that he had 'seen some Shakespeare'. A Macready-pause ensued. Then the reply: 'You wouldn't have *seen* much . . . but I hope you listened'.

Though listening in a period of assorted background noises might seem to be a dying habit, our classical companies cannot grumble. Audiences at the National and Royal Shakespeare Theatres—not to speak of the new St. George's—are informed and eager. Certainly they do not let the plays wash over them; in general, the level of interpretation and response is as high as it has been for a very long time. Of course, great actors in great parts have invariably made their own laws. Dame Rebecca West, in a parenthesis on Henry Irving, said in effect that though he was so often inaudible during his later years, 'the melodic line of his murmurs . . . never failed to evoke the truth' about Shylock.

When I was first going to the play, minor actors would lose themselves again and again in unintelligently sonorous booming. That, I hope, is over. Certainly today we are likely to get the sense with the sound. Euphronius will not toss away

> I was of late as petty to his ends
> As is the morn-dew on the myrtle-leaf
> To his grand sea

or the Welsh Captain fumble round with

> The bay-trees in our country are all withered,
> And meteors fright the fixed stars of heaven

or a Second Gentleman smother

> The wind-shak'd surge, with high and monstrous mane,
> Seems to cast water on the burning Bear,
> And quench the guards of th' ever fixed Pole.

But these are the merest footnotes to the imperial theme. An American patriot, praising Shakespeare judiciously, is said to have exclaimed: 'Not more than three people in this city could have written the plays'. Let me say that it would be an enviable audience that had in it three such listeners as Martin Holmes. Readers of his previous books[1] know that he has a hearing granted to very few. For him the smallest speeches are burnished. A pebble is powdered suddenly with glinting mica. We remember Cibber on Betterton: 'In the delivery of Poetical Numbers . . . it is scarce credible upon how minute an Article of Sound depends their greatest Beauty or Inaffection'. I think, too, of Christopher Fry's words, in another context, upon a music that

> Looping and threading, tuning and entwining,
> Flings a babel of bells, a carolling,
> Of such various vowels that the ear can almost feel
> The soul of sound when it lay in chaos yearning
> For the tongue to be created.

The soul of sound . . . Without (I hope) standing too long in your way, I invite your attention to Mr. Holmes's remarkable book, his study of Shakespeare's diction and melodic line, his infallible ear for a cadence, his discussion of the Shakespeare-Burbage partnership, his analysis of such a showpiece of the Theatre Theatrical as *Richard III*. Shakespeare, writing at speed, could hear every line superbly in the mind.

To read this book is to have our own minds sharpened. In service as a drama critic I recall speech upon speech as they were spoken—at the time, it appeared, definitively: names are immaterial. But definition is a dangerous word; there must always be room for a fresh revelation. 'We'll hear a play', said Hamlet, and Mr. Holmes's readers will find surprising excitement when they return to this play or the other for a second time or a fiftieth. Thanks to him, they can hear it now in the deep heart's core.

J. C. TREWIN

[1]*Shakespeare's Public; The Guns of Elsinore; Shakespeare and His Players.*

Chapter One

SOUND BEFORE SENSE

A SPOKEN PHRASE of any significance makes its initial impression by sound. The sense may follow almost immediately, but it is the cadence of words rightly chosen that makes a passage linger in the mind long enough for its meaning to be comprehended and carry the maximum of effect. Expressed in less judiciously-selected words a sentence may be a matter of narrative, exhortation, or description, but it will flow on its way unremarked, and, like Prospero's 'insubstantial pageant' in *The Tempest,* leave not a wrack behind. Even on the written page its impact will be neglibible, and the reader will repeatedly find himself obliged to turn back and read paragraph or page once more from its beginning if he is to be sure of the essential meaning the words are intended to convey.

This is particularly noticeable in the study of Elizabethan English, both in prose and verse. A public lately and traditionally illiterate was advancing, step by rapid step, towards full and effective literacy, but was dominated, in the process, by the sound and sense of words read, sung or declaimed by others, and still absorbed the sense through the sounds uttered by the tongue, rather than by the appearance of words written or printed on a page. With the writings of divines, University lecturers or politicians, it was a natural feature of their ordinary technique as employed from pulpit or platform, and prose writers unversed in this oral tradition were apt to be dull and less immediately effective for the lack of it. The prose of Holinshed's *Chronicle* is inclined to be tedious in places, where it is not transcribing the text of the preacher William Harrison, the Parliamentary speaker Edward Hall, or that great jurist and orator, St. Thomas More, but a generation later, with the spread of classical learning among ordinary laymen, it is noteworthy how many writers are influenced, consciously or otherwise, by the balanced style of Tacitus. Open Speed's *Chronicle* at random, and cadence after cadence will challenge the attention of eye and ear alike, as if the work were designed expressly for reading aloud; the splendid prose of the Authorised Version of the Bible is expressly presented as 'appointed to be read in churches', Ralegh's *History of the World,* despite its incompleteness, inconsequence and a phenomenally idiotic index, fascinates the reader by the sheer pleasure of its phrasing, and the style perhaps reaches its culmination in the noble periods of Sir Thomas Browne.

Even more than preacher, chronicler or rhetorician, the dramatist was affected by these considerations of sound. Where others used it to express their own arguments or personalities, he had the chance of making it serve both these and other ends. Judiciously employed, it could differentiate one character from another, situation from situation and even mood from mood, and no Elizabethan or Jacobean dramatist realised these possibilities so fully, or exploited them so effectively, as William Shakespeare, from the time when he found himself working in close and continued association with Richard Burbage, and with the theatre Burbage's father had built. Poet, player and playhouse formed a combination that brought out the best qualities of all three, and all three came to an end within little over a single hand-count of years of each other, but before that day they had served each other for some 20 years in an alliance that has never been surpassed, or even equalled, in English theatrical history.

The name of Burbage is associated in most people's minds with the fact that he was Shakespeare's leading actor for the greater part of his career. We attribute his unquestioned renown, in his own time and in subsequent tradition, to the excellence of the parts that Shakespeare wrote for him, but we have paid less attention, hitherto, to the possibility of his own influence on Shakespeare and, in especial, on Shakespeare's use of language. It is a point that can bear with rather more consideration than it has yet received.

Burbage's voice, it would seem, was not a trumpet like Alleyn's, but had more of the quality of a stringed instrument, and Shakespeare wrote for it with consideration and full understanding of its potentialities. There is a marked change, accordingly, from the lines devised for Alleyn's declamation at the Rose on Bankside to those with which Burbage was to win, and retain, the admiration of the patrons of his father's two theatres in Finsbury Fields. Moreover, one of the new actor's gifts, probably inborn, but certainly fostered by his early training, was versatility. This comes more easily to a light voice than to a consistently heavy one, and examination of Shakespeare's work suggests that he appreciated this quality from the first, and made judicious and effective use of it. Ben Jonson, when his turn came, exploited it enthusiastically, but with far less subtlety, in parts such as Brainworm in *Every Man in his Humour,* Face in *The Alchemist,* and most of all, perhaps, in that ingenious Venetian who gives his name to *Volpone.*

Consideration of voice and versatility had their effect on Shakespeare's style, and a detailed study of his plays enables us to trace the development of author and actor alike, from the youthful virtuosity of Berowne, the first product of their alliance, to the complex characters of Coriolanus and Henry VIII.

Readers with long memories may be reminded of a similar exercise carried out some 15 years back, inviting consideration of the plays in the light of the audiences for which they were written, and may feel at the outset that they are being taken over familiar ground. So, in a sense, they are, but it is ground worth traversing again for a different purpose. Where certain points of cadence, in the earlier study, served to differentiate one character from another, deeper investigation in one single character—usually that of the principal figure—indicates a variation between mood and mood, and by affecting the actual pace of the dialogue provides us with a deeper insight into the original intention of the play, so that matter that was not always relevant to the main issue in the first instance may prove interesting and not unrewarding in its present context. To such readers, if any, I offer my apologies for anything that may seem repetitious, and my good wishes for their enjoyment of anything that may tempt them to further consideration and conjecture on their own.

Chapter Two

TWO STARS RISING

WHEN SHAKESPEARE first began to write plays for the company known as the Chamberlain's Men, in 1593 or 1594, their leading player was Richard Burbage, a son of that James Burbage who had been a pioneer of theatrical enterprise in London about 20 years earlier. In 1576 James had set up, in Finsbury Fields, the first known playhouse in the country, and his sons, as they grew up, had followed the theatrical profession as a matter of course. Richard, the youngest, was born in 1568, and was therefore a boy of eight when his father launched this new and fascinating venture, which meant that throughout his career he had the advantage over his fellows of a longer experience of life in and around a permanent theatre. Its advantages and its problems were different from those of the 'fit-ups' who travelled from place to place, or gave their performances from time to time in town halls or inn-yards. A building of solid timber had its own hazards—notably that of fire, by which its remains were ultimately to perish—but it was a fixed, permanent home and headquarters, and that was something that the English theatre had never had before. Audiences in future were to come to *it,* instead of its having to pick up its assorted luggage and go out to them, and the players were to exercise their art, and display their talents, on their own ground and very much on their own terms. It marked a tremendous advance in theatrical conditions and theatrical opportunities, and in those conditions, and in full sight of those opportunities, the boy grew up.

And, as he grew up and developed, the art and craft of the theatre was growing and developing all around him. The substitution of a fixed theatre for a touring one meant that the time fomerly spent in travelling was now available for rehearsal, preparation and much more fully-detailed production. A play might now be planned and written not only for a particular company of actors, but for the resources of a particular stage. It would still be wise to avoid effects that might be difficult or impossible elsewhere—touring was not completely abandoned, and the company might be called upon to fulfil specific engagements in this great house or that, if patrons were interested and encouraging—but from the very outset the author, actors and manager would be able to imagine the effect of scene after scene, entry after entry, sensation after sensation, in terms of the actual stage on which it was to be performed.

The change may justly be said to have revolutionsed the art of the theatre in England. It had its effect, as time went on, upon authors, actors, managers and the theatre-going public in general, and not least—though no one would notice it at the time—on a small boy in a theatrical family, destined for the theatrical profession as a matter of course. There were all kinds of odd jobs, errands and miscellaneous duties about the building that would be relegated to 'the boy', just as if he were an apprentice in a London shop, and like the London apprentice, he grew up in close association with a definite, firmly-built structure that stood at once for his profession and his home. This association with the fabric of the Theatre, and familiarity with the stage, the galleries—quite possibly he had had to sweep them in his time—the tower, the tiring-house and the dusty depths under the stage where the furniture was kept, gave him a background that his elders lacked. Their world had been something much more like that of the circus artiste; his, even before he was allowed to appear as a boy-actor, was that of the stage.

We need not be surprised, then, that when he came to his maturity he was so far ahead of his contemporaries. The simple fact was that he had come to the profession, in its new form, earlier in life, and been at work longer, than they. Much of what he knew had been learnt the hard way, but he knew more about that particular theatre, in all its aspects, than any later recruit to the company, and that fact was important, because for some time it was the only theatre there was. The very fact that he had been the youngest son, the odd-job-boy who might be given any kind of work to do, or to assist in, meant that he could hardly avoid getting a broad general impression of what was being done, and what had to be done, in all the various aspects of his father's business. As time went on and his talent had scope for exercise, the natural progression was from odd-job-boy and son-of-the-house to boy-player, and in due course to boy-actress. There is good reason to think his voice was not of the thundrous type, and there would be a pleasant period, before it broke, when he could play girls' parts as well as pages and boys brought in, as on Pompey's galley in *Antony and Cleopatra* or the pages in *As You Like It,* to vary proceedings with a song.

Another point worth bearing in mind is that this position as son of the proprietor gave him a chance of knowing, and being known by, the general acting profession of his time. His father, now that he had practically abandoned acting for management, let out his new playhouse to such different companies as had the enterprise, and the money, to rent it from him, and the young Burbages presumably 'went with the house' as permanent staff available for such work as might be required, on the stage or off it. Besides the Queen's Men, there were other companies of players, under the patronage of various noblemen; they appeared, played in London or at the Theatre, toured up and down the country, dissolving as their noble patrons died or lost interest. James Burbage found it worth while to build an extra house—the Curtain—to accommodate them, and soon Philip Henslowe, dyer and moneylender, was following his example and managing the Rose on Bankside and another playhouse at Newington Butts.

Here, perhaps, is the explanation of a point long at issue between those two great Shakespearean scholars, Sir Edmund Chambers and Sir Walter Greg. Chambers maintained that the companies called the Admiral's Men and the Lord Strange's Men were practically amalgamated by 1590 or thereabouts. Greg, on the other hand, claimed that they worked in alliance, but that each retained its own identity and very much of its own organisation, the Admiral's Men

being based on the Theatre and Strange's on the Curtain
near by, with Richard Burbage playing indifferently for both
of them. When Chambers writes, 'I know no other contemporary example of an actor playing concurrently for two
companies',[1] he is unconsciously illustrating Richard's unique
position at the time. He was an obviously talented young
man in his early twenties, he was the son of the proprietor
of both theatres and available for engagement at one or the
other, according to the arrangements made with the hirers.
Very much the same sort of thing was still current in living
memory when touring companies, as distinct from single
productions on tour, took a stock of pieces up and down
the country. Usually they visited places where they were
known, and where they knew the theatres and resources
available and could select their repertoire accordingly. Frank
Benson and Henry Baynton with Shakespeare, and Carl Rosa,
Edward Denhoff and Joseph O'Mara with grand opera are
perhaps the best-remembered examples. Usually they took
with them their cast of principals, their scenery and properties
and a nucleus of chorus and orchestra, engaging auxiliaries
and 'extras' from the theatres themselves and sometimes
doing much the same in the matter of scenery. (Sir John
Martin-Harvey in his autobiography[2] describes the stock
'palace arches', gardens and kitchen settings with which they
were sometimes confronted in his early training days, and
which had to serve for practically everything.) One result
of this system was a particular relationship achieved between
the members of the company and the permanent staff of
the provincial theatres which they visited season after season.
Each got to know the tastes, capactities and shortcomings of
the other, and to co-operate, as a matter of course, in producing performances which would be to the credit, and the
financial advantage, of players and theatre-management alike.
   All this would serve as an excellent training for young
Richard. He would have to do all kinds of work, and meet
all kinds of people—including Edward Alleyn, a year or

[1] Chambers,*William Shakespeare* (Oxford, Clarendon Press, 1930), I, 51,
[2] *The Autobiography of Sir John Martin-Harvey* (London, Sampson
    Low, Marston & Co., 1933), pp. 122–23.

two older than he and soon to consolidate his position by marrying his manager's step-daughter and becoming the star actor of the Admiral's Men—and to be able to get on with all of them on reasonably friendly terms. Properly used, as it is clear that he used them, these opportunities constituted an invaluable training in versatility, and versatility was one of his great characteristics in later life, as appears from the parts that Shakespeare wrote for him when he had become, for the Chamberlain's Men, what Alleyn was for the Admiral's. Alleyn had a fine, resonant voice and a commanding presence, and played on these for all they were worth, eventually going into management, where they would still have been of good service to him. Burbage, by contrast, seems to have carried less weight, but to have had a wider range, and longer experience, of the varieties of human emotion, owing to that apprenticeship of having to be all things to all men in the various productions given in his father's theatre.

With such a background it is not surprising that he included painting among his accomplishments. We know that in 1613 he and Shakespeare were called upon to design and provide a pageant-shield with an emblematic device for the Earl of Rutland to carry in the course of the king's accession-day festivities. Shakespeare did the 'devising' and Burbage the 'making and painting', and the latter was called on again three years later to paint another, possibly a fresh treatment of Shakespeare's design. It looks as if the theatre-boy's early experiences in the joinery-and-decorating line were bearing fruit.

When the original Theatre was under construction, the whole Burbage family had set their hands to it in one way or another—not only James himself, who had been a joiner and came to it naturally, but his wife's brother, John Brayne (a well-to-do grocer, who had put up the capital), and, we may imagine somewhat resentfully, Mrs. Brayne, who had to do her share of manual work when they could not afford paid labour. General painting and decorating might be left (under supervision) to the small boy, especially if he proved to have a taste and talent for that sort of thing. The Rutland commission shows that he continued with it in later life, and he has always been credited not only with the portrait of himself at Dulwich (Plate I), but with practically all the still-extant likenesses of his stage contemporaries, including the portrait of Shakespeare engraved by Martin Droeshout for the First Folio and, with much less likelihood, the 'Chandos' portrait, a work of very different style and dubious pedigree. (Sir William Davenant, who owned it in the 17th century, was ready to cast aspersions on his mother's honesty in order to support the gossip that he was a natural son of Shakespeare, and he would not have scrupled to back the rumour with a bogus 'family portrait' of someone with more beard and less brow than the Droeshout engraving or the Stratford memorial bust—the only two contemporarily-accepted likenesses.)

Long before this, however, there had been trouble among the management. The Brayne-Burbage partnership had not run smoothly. James Burbage, as the only professional woodworker of the family, had paid himself a salary out of the funds available, regarding the rest of them as unskilled, unprofessional assistants, and when the theatre was a going concern, his business integrity was roundly questioned. He was said to have a duplicate key to the strong-box and to be helping himself from it in secret, and to have concealed some of the gate-money about his own person instead of putting it into the box at all. When Brayne died, his widow demanded a half share in all the gross takings. When she could not get it out of Burbage by written application, she came along to the theatre with a rather disreputable supporter named Miles and a nonentity named Bishop to serve as a witness, and raised all the trouble she could. Young Richard, then in his very early twenties, belaboured Miles with a broomstick and tweaked Bishop's nose, while his father leaned out of an upstairs window and shouted unseemly epithets at the complainants.

Some months later, James had a furious quarrel in the tiring-room with the Admiral's Men, swearing 'with a great oath' that he cared nothing for them, nor the Admiral, their patron, nor for three of the best lords of them all. After that, they left the Theatre and played elsewhere, eventually settling at the Rose on Bankside. It was only then that

Henslowe began the diary and account-books that are still preserved in Alleyn's foundation of Dulwich College and provide such valuable information about the theatres of their day, so it is not surprising that there is nothing in them about the Burbages. On the other hand, it is there that we find our first indication of Shakespeare's arrival in the world of the theatre—and, at the same moment, of his effect upon it. On 3 March, 1592, a play called 'Harey the vi' was performed at the Rose by Lord Strange's Men, and made a lot of money. The sign 'ne' against it in Henslowe's diary indicates that it was new; the fact that it was played again in a few days' time, and continued to draw good audiences, shows that it was successful. The diarist does not trouble to record who wrote it—that, in a table of box-office returns, was hardly a relevant matter—but it can be identified as Shakespeare's *First Part of King Henry the Sixth*. Henslowe, and Lord Strange's Men, had got hold of a new author, and a potentially profitable one.

There was at one time an almost frantic tendency, on the part of Shakespeare scholars, to pull the early plays to pieces—particularly this one—and attribute different passages, sometimes whole scenes, sometimes speeches of comparatively few lines only, to other playwrights on the grounds of the unquestionable variation of style noticeable in the text. Nowadays, however, this elaborate disintegration is largely abandoned in favour of the simpler and quite logical theory that Shakespeare, in his early days, had not yet developed a style of his own, and began, not unnaturally, by imitating other people's, principally those to be heard in the theatre where he worked. The result is a jumble of experiments, not always very successful, just as the play itself is a jumble of incidents and ideas. Apparently the author is not yet sure of what he is doing, or how to set his ideas in order, but he has from the beginning an inborn mastery of effective sound.

It is easy, in these days, to overlook the tremendous importance of sound in the theatres which Burbage was building and for which Shakespeare was writing. The editors of the First Folio, seven years after his death, urged the importance of reading the plays again and again if one were to understand them and get full enjoyment from them. Later editors met the reader still further by adding indications of locality at the beginning of each scene, and these accretions, not always accurate when judged by Shakespeare's own text, have come to be taken for granted, and to be relied on, albeit unconsciously, when we read the plays. Modern productions often include elaborate programme-notes, instructing the spectator how he should approach the performance, and from what aspect he should consider the play in the light of modern ethics and ideas. All these things are now common form, some of them are helpful and many of them serve ends which the author himself must have thought desirable in his own time. But, in his own time, he had to serve those ends without the means afforded to later editors, playwrights, and producers, and so readily taken for granted. The plays were not in print, available to be read by the interested playgoer before attending the performance, or contemplatively on returning home. Once a play was in print, that meant that anybody could buy it, and other managements could act it, so it was to the interest of the author and the company *not* to have the text published until its immediate popularity was over. *King Richard II* was published (in a discreetly expurgated text) in quarto form in 1597 and 1598, when the plays with Falstaff in them had pushed it into the background, and when Sir Gilly Meyrick wanted to commission a revival of it in 1601 the players complained that it was 'so old and so out of use' that hardly anybody would come. That, in fact, was what had made it worthwhile to publish it as reading-matter, to reach a different public, or the same public in a different, more contemplative mood.

A new play, on the contrary, had to make itself immediately acceptable and interesting with very few resources. Visually there was little that could be done. The stage, at the beginning, would look very much as it always had looked, the appearance of the opening characters would depend very much on the extent and variety of the theatre wardrobe. An actor coming on to that stage has to lose no time in indicating to the audience who he is, where he is and what he is doing there, or the audience will feel

puzzled, impatient and vaguely resentful, and the play will
have put it in the wrong mood at the very beginning. We are
so familiar with the story and text of *Macbeth*, for instance,
that the little opening scene has lost much of its original
dramatic force. To an audience coming to a new play and not
knowing what to expect, it gives not only atmosphere, but
information. There is word of a battle, of a heath, of somebody called Macbeth who is shortly to appear, and a sinister
hint that when he does so he will find something unexpected
and rather unpleasant waiting for him. No sooner are we
conscious of this than the speakers have taken flight, leaving
us in an uneasy, apprehensive mood, and the real action of
the play begins. And it has all been done for us by the choice
of a few words, and the sound of them in our ears, conveying
information and interest at once. This, as we shall see, is the
practice throughout all Shakespeare's plays, but it is of
particular importance at the beginning.

Where Marlowe starts *Tamburlaine the Great* with a weak
and querulous character saying 'Brother Cosroe, I find myself
aggrieved', Shakespeare opens *Henry VI* with a ringing
monosyllable that can sound through the auditorium like
a gong, and jerk the chattering, apple-eating spectators into
involuntary attention as readily as the theatre's trumpeter
in his tower.

> Hung be the heavens with black. Yield, day, to night,
> Comets, importing change of times and states
> Brandish your crystal tresses in the sky
> And with them scourge the bad revolting stars
> That have consented unto Henry's death!

The new author seems to be writing imitation Marlowe, and
very good Marlowe at that. It is declamation, rhodomontade
perhaps, but the lines in this very extravagance embody the
mourning of a nation at the loss of a hero-king.

In a very few moments we are confronted with the main
theme. The mourning nobles fall to argument and recrimination, by the means of a succession of messengers we learn
how their neglect of affairs abroad is leading to the disintegration of the great possessions in France, and this news
in turn leads to further accusation, counter-accusation and

Figure 1.—Assault on a city by artillery, musketry, hand-to-hand combat in a breach of the wall and, in the far distance, an attack with scaling-ladders. A frequently-repeated illustration in Holinshed's *Chronicle*, 1577, showing the image likely to be called to the spectators' minds by Shakespeare's dialogue and off-stage noises in the scenes at Orleans and Rouen in *I Henry VI* and later in the Harfleur scenes of *Henry V*.

intrigue. It is the eternal story of a house divided against itself, as Shakespeare was to elaborate it in his great cycle depicting the rise and fall of the House of Lancaster, and in the earlier, isolated story of King John.

But at this point all sorts of other ideas come crowding in. The author may have felt, or well-meaning colleagues may have said, that 'the play wants action, my boy—action!', and accordingly the music of the words is abandoned for the clash of swords, the visual effect of men—and a young woman—hurrying about in armour, and a sudden sensation-scene with the discharge of an unseen cannon. With the change of subject comes a change of style. Shakespeare is imitating different models, and writing, deliberately or instinctively, in the mode of each in turn, while at intervals his own original idea breaks through, with the quarrels and intrigues of the opposing English factions. Even a character can be made to suffer this dichotomy: Joan the Maid, at her first appearance, has a radiance that seems to make her out as the guardian saint of France, but by the end she is more like Marlowe's Faustus in her scene with the spirits, and before her judges in her last scene of all she is speaking inferior Marlowe in the style of *The Massacre at Paris*. There are other experiments in verse-form, like the dying Mortimer's scene of exposition on the one hand and the rhymed, rhythmical dialogue of the Talbots—formal, but unexpectedly effective—on the other, and the main theme is brought in to reconcile the two distinct dramas that seem to be going on at the same time when the quarrel between the English leaders, resulting in the death of Talbot, foreshadows the way in which the rivalry of Lancaster and York is to go near to accomplishing the destruction of England. When Shakespeare wrote elsewhere about the dyer's hand being 'subdued to what it works in' he knew very well what he was talking about.

It is permissible to guess that this play, hotch-potch as it is, did not have to wait for its first night to be recognised as a potential success. There was far more money taken at the doors than had been recorded for weeks, and one must bear in mind that this large audience had come in, and had paid to come in, before it had had a chance of seeing the play at all. Somehow, be it by good publicity or simple report of its effectiveness and excitement in rehearsal, the Bankside playgoer had gained an impression that he was going to get his money's worth. Even before the play was finished, the author must have been given heartening assurance that his colleagues and employers believed in it, were convinced of its success and intended it to be the first of many. We may even wonder if the very last scene was played, or even written, at the time of that first performance. Without it, Suffolk's capture of Margaret of Anjou, and his use of her as an instrument in coming to terms with France, would serve to round off the play with a proper patriotic finale,

> So, now dismiss your army when ye please,
> Hang up your ensigns, let your drums be still,
> For here we entertain a solemn peace.

On the other hand, we may be sure that if the play originated without that following scene, it did not have to wait for it long. The scene takes the action, and the time, a step forward, and ends with an indication of more to come, in the old serial-story fashion of 'To be continued in our next'. It leads straight on to the opening of the play known as the *Second Part of King Henry VI,* and that again leads on to the *Third Part*, as if there were no more than an act-interval between. By this time the author has got his ideas under control and can go ahead, writing the play as he wants to write it, not as he thinks other people may think he ought to write it. Instead of writing like Marlowe, Kyd, Peele, Greene, or Nash in turns, he is writing much more consistently like Shakespeare, and this leads on to a suggestion that is admittedly conjectural but may explain much.

Henslowe's diary records 15 performances between March and June 1592. This, for a new play by an unknown writer, is fantastic. Those old favourites, Kyd's *Spanish Tragedy* and Marlowe's *Jew of Malta,* come nearest to it, over the same period, with 12 and 10 performances respectively, and the less familiar *Muley Mollocco* (probably Peele's *Battle of Alcazar*) with another ten. Henslowe was a shrewd business man, and it is doubtful whether one new play could have attracted audiences enough to fill the theatre 15 times over in a short season, and still more doubtful whether Henslowe could ever have thought it would. Rather more in character is the conclusion that he had seen in that first play an initial success that was worth following up at once by carrying on the story in a sequel—indeed, as it turned out, by making it as a serial, so that the audience in each play would be encouraged to come again and see what happened next.

A young man brim-full of ideas can write fast when he has to, and sometimes writes all the better for it. The remaining plays of the cycle are far better constructed than the first one, because the author has had less time to think out what, by his fellows' example, he ought to put in, and enough success and encouragement to justify him in going on with the play he originally wanted to write. The theme of mutual envy, mistrust and antagonism, evident in the first scene of the first play, is now carried on without irrelevant interruptions. In the second it is a matter of plot

and counterplot, conspiracy and intrigue, and in the third
it is working itself out almost exclusively by force of arms.
The battles this time are not put in as sensation-scenes;
they indicate the fluctuating course of the war, fortune
favouring this side or that, and in one formal but unforget-
table scene the misery and waste that such war can cause in
the lives of ordinary simple men.

These two later plays are so well integrated with each
other, and so much better than their forerunner, that they
were soon able to be independent of it, and to do without
it entirely. Our knowledge of contemporary events, and of
Elizabethan practice and present-day echoes of it, enables
us to piece out, from the evidence, what almost certainly
happened. It began when some London apprentices, resenting
the imprisonment of one of their number in the Marshalsea,
organised a prison-breaking party and made the Rose their
rendezvous before setting out on their attempt at rescue.
There was a riot, and an enquiry, and though the players
themselves had been in no way to blame, the authorities
determined to teach the playgoers of Southwark a sharp
lesson. They had the playhouse closed down till Michaelmas,
and Henslowe's summer season came to an abrupt end.

The course to follow, in such an event, was to go on tour
for a while, and that is what Alleyn and his colleagues duly
did. An upheaval like this, however, might be made the
occasion for changes in the company itself. Not all the
resident players might be wanted 'on the road', not all of
them would want to go, and it might be preferable, in the
eyes of some, to seek employment with another company,
which had not got itself into trouble. Such a company came
into being in 1592-3 under the patronage of the Earl of
Pembroke, and included in its repertory two plays based
on the Second and Third Parts of *Henry* I. The texts are
extant in quarto form, and the title-pages of both are
significant in different ways, both of them worthy of
consideration.

The earlier of the two, a crude version of the *Second Part
of King Henry VI,* claims to be the *First Part of the Contention betwixt the two famous Houses of Yorke and Lancaster.*
The lines of Suffolk and Lord Scales are given with reasonable

accuracy, Scales in his few lines being practically word-perfect, but the scenes in which they do not appear, and which they would have had no occasion to watch at rehearsal, are reconstructed on the gag-and-guesswork principle familiar to students of the Bad Quartos in general. An actor has come to the company with personal recollections of a new play or two that drew good money when he was with his last management. He remembers his own lines, or most of them, and the lines spoken near him when he was on the stage, or just round the corner, waiting for his cue to enter. With these, and other people's recollections of the plays in performance, it should be possible to reconstruct something, at least, of the scenes which took place while he was out of sight in the tiring-house and, if the play had been a money-maker on tour, to have the text of this acting version printed, and sell it as an original. The bold assertion that the play is 'The *First* Part' of the contention shows that the true first part had been simply discarded. Its form would have made it more difficult to reconstruct from half-remembered scenes and speeches, whereas the other two plays were more straightforward and could do quite well without it. The old Third Part appears as *The True Tragedy of Richard Duke of York,* and the title-page of the Quarto (printed in the next year, 1595) contains the words 'as it was sundry times acted by the Right Honourable the Earl of Pembroke his Servants'.

Accepting this interpretation of Henslowe's box-office entries, we find events coming out in a logical order. Shakespeare's first play is successful enough to be given two more performances in the next 10 days. He is encouraged to carry on the story, and the next play is ready for production just over three weeks after the success of the first. (This is by no means impossible; Anthony Munday is noted in the Henslowe papers as contracting to provide a play within the next fortnight, and more than one contemporary has paid tribute to the facility with which Shakespeare wrote.) There is no need for Henslowe to record the next play in his diary as a Second Part; when he did that with *Tamar Cam* the case was different, because the First Part was no longer in the current repertory and it was as well to note that this was a new play, not a revival. The Third Part would have been taking shape in the poet's mind while the Second was coming from his pen, and would not be long in following. Thereafter we find two sets of three performances played at intervals of about a week, one on April 5, 13 and 21, and the next on May 4, 9 and 16. Then come two pairs of performances on May 22 and 29, and, after a longer interval, on June 12 and 20. One may at least claim to read in this a strong suggestion that *Henry VI* was being played as a cycle, in the manner of Wagner's *Ring des Nibelungen,* with extra performances of the two later plays of the cycle, even as the *Ring* is occasionally followed by isolated performances of *Die Walküre* and *Götterdämmerung.*

This would explain the resentment of Robert Greene, and the tirade, in his *Groat's worth of Wit,* against

> an upstart Crow, beautified with our feathers, that with his *Tygers hart wrapt in a Players hyde* supposes he is as well able to bombast out a blanke verse as the best of you: and being an absolute *Johannes fac totum,* is in his owne conceit the onely Shake-scene in a countrey.

Greene died in the autumn of 1592, and it has been difficult heretofore to account for his parodying a line out of the *Third Part of King Henry VI* if Henslowe's entries refer to the First Part only. Grant that all three parts were in existence, and in performance, by the preceding summer, and the difficulty vanishes, while Greene's bitterness becomes even easier to understand. The anonymous writer of the *Parnassus* plays was to put the position tersely and clearly in a sentence given to Kempe:

> Few of the University men pen plaies well, they smell too much of that writer *Ovid* and that writer *Metamorphosis*, and talke too much of *Proserpina* and *Juppiter*. Why heres our fellow *Shakespeare* puts them all downe, I and *Ben Ionson* too.

Greene was a University man, a literary man, and a failure; Shakespeare was a provincial, a common player, and a success, and that was both incomprehensible and unforgivable.

Players were there to speak the lines that educated men had written for them, not to write plays on their own account and put the poets out of business. Dissolute, penniless and dying, the unsuccessful poet voiced his grievance in a pamphlet published after his death by Henry Chettle, his literary executor, who regretted it a little later, when he had met Shakespeare personally and found he liked him. In *Kind-Harts Dreame*, published three months later, he utters a handsome disclaimer and a tribute to the actor-writer's personal character and professional reputation.

Meanwhile the Bankside riots and the closing of the theatre had put a stop to Henslowe's season of performances by Lord Strange's Men. They went into the provinces, and somebody fell away from that company and ultimately joined Pembroke's, enabling them to get up their garbled version of *Henry VI*. Finally, when for one reason or another it had outlived its usefulness as an acting play, they had it printed, ingeniously wording the titles of the two parts so that the unwary purchaser might think he had the orthodox original versions, and that any others, such as Lord Strange's people might put out in rivalry, were no more than spurious imitations. The policy seems to have worked; a company (presumably Strange's, from their general repertory) produced *Henry VI* apparently on January 16 and 30, 1593, but that is all, and thereafter we hear of it no more. Francis Meres does not include it in the list of Shakespeare's plays which he cites in his *Palladis Tamia*, published in 1598, and we may justifiably assume that by that time it had become obsolete. Indeed, it may well have done so before Meres came to London at all, as he was at the University till 1593, and Shakespeare had written much, and much better, in the course of the next five years.

The playing and publication of the corrupt Henry VI play may have impaired the usefulness of the genuine trilogy, but the author was not long in providing a substitute. A generation or two ago, critics had no words too strong to revile *Titus Andronicus* as revolting in theme, extravagant in action, turgid in style, unbalanced in construction, and quite obviously not by Shakespeare. Recent revivals over the last half-century, principally Olivier's memorable Titus, Anthony Quayle's Aaron, and Maxine Audley's vengeful Tamora, have shown the fallacy of these facile condemnations. It was written for the stage, not the study, and on the stage, when played by actors of sufficient calibre and technique, the fustian takes on a terrifying grandeur. The late Wilfrid Walter, at the Old Vic in Robert Atkins's production of 1923–24, was the first Titus of modern times; possibly the first since the author's death to play the part as the author wrote it. The 17th and 18th centuries preferred the version adapted by Edward Ravenscroft, who explained his short way with Shakespeare by producing, perhaps even originating, the legend that the play had in fact been written by somebody else, who had persuaded Shakespeare to put his name to it and add a few finishing touches.

Atkins went back to the original, and insisted, in this as in all his productions, on clear, natural diction that gave full value to the music of Shakespeare's lines. Consciously or unconsciously, he produced the play in the season following the one in which he had put on the three parts of *Henry VI,* and the transition was all the easier in consequence for the players concerned. Think of the first act for a moment or two in a 15th-century setting, and at once we might be back among the quarrels, rivalries and intrigues of Somerset and York, with Margaret substituted for Tamora and Titus coming home from the wars like Talbot and then being under-valued and slighted like Humphrey of Gloucester. At this stage, at any rate, it is still very much the same sort of play, written by the same man, to be acted by the same people. Aaron the 'Moor' (an unmistakeable negro, both from the text and from Henry Peacham's contemporary drawing at Longleat) has stood silent and impressive throughout the whole first scene, but he opens the second act alone, with a speech that seems vaguely familiar after the other play, not in the words themselves so much as the style, sound and character of the man who speaks them. A little more, and we may recognise him as the Suffolk of *Henry VI* with his face blacked. Further than that, two of Suffolk's lines in the first scene with Margaret

> She's beautiful, and therefore to be wooed,
> She is a woman, therefore to be won,

actually recur, with a slight variation, in Aaron's first scene, though this time they are given to Demetrius. Aaron goes on to further enormities in the course of the play, but his extravagance of language has had a parallel in Suffolk's curses at the prospect of his banishment. Both parts have the same kind of verbal music and were written in the same key, so we may be justified in assuming that they were originally written for the same actor.

Titus himself is an obvious Alleyn part, extravagance and all, from his first well-prepared entry with the ringing words, 'Hail, Rome', to the cannibalistic banquet at the end, where the dignity and sonority of the players have to hold the audience transfixed and spellbound until the tension is relieved by sudden action. Citing the example of the Roman patriarch Virginius, who killed his daughter in the days of the Republic, he first induces Saturninus to approve the principle and then puts it into practice by himself, stabbing the veiled Lavinia, with the words

> Die, die, Lavinia, and thy shame with thee
> And with thy shame thy father's sorrow die!

The dialogue now continues almost exclusively in rhymed couplets, and the effect is not that of a jingle, but of a heightened tension and solemnity, the rhyming word falling into place by right not only of sound but of natural, inevitable consequence. When Titus reveals his daughter's dishonour and mutilation, and Saturninus bids him 'tell who did the deed' his immediate response is apparently quite irrelevant, and is addressed to Tamora. 'Will't please you eat? will't please your highness feed?' he says, as if he did not want to let trivialities interrupt the meal. The spectators know what it is that she is eating, and appreciate the terrible appropriateness of the rhyming word. Meanwhile, Titus has named the ravishers, still in the formality of stately couplets. Saturinus breaks in with the swift, indignant command, 'Go, fetch them higher to us presently', to be met with an instant answer, 'Why, there they are both'. It is a moment for Saturninus to look sharply round among the assembled company, until he realises where Titus's eyes and knife are pointing. Then comes the terrible rhyming word, and the couplet inexorably detailing the horror,

> baked in that pie
> Whereof their mother daintily hath fed
> Eating the flesh that she herself hath bred.

As is to counter the general incredulity, and to produce convincing proof, he goes on quite calmly and reassuringly, ''Tis true, 'tis true, witness my knife's sharp point', and before anyone can fully realise what he is saying, the knife is in Tamora's body and she lies dead or dying over the remains of her sons. The stately formality of rhyme, that has kept us at one remove from revulsion, has been snapped like an over-tuned string by the use of one sudden, unemphatic word with no rhyme to it, and a gesture that brings us abruptly to the realism of death. Next moment we are called back to the saving artificiality of word-music; there are two more killings in the next three lines of verse, and all three lines rhyme. Saturninus, cheek-by-jowl with Titus and Tamora, is close enough for an instant reaction. Vowel and consonant together seem to mark the exact moment of the stroke, and the second half of the line gives the reaction and justification for it,

> Die, frantic wretch, for this accursed deed.

Lucius Andronicus would not be immediately close to them on the stage; one needs a moment or two for the spectators, in the play and in the audience alike, to realise what has happened, and so violence is not immediately succeeded by violence. This time the line suggests not action, but a moment of absolute stillness and amazement

> Can the son's eye behold his father bleed?

Next moment comes a line of violent action, stroke after stroke thudding in with alliteration of vowel-rhyme and consonant to emphase it,

> There's meed for meed, death for a deadly deed.

Deliberately or not, Shakespeare has handled the scene in such a way as to give the audience something to listen to, and thereby to distract their minds from undue consideration of what they see. He has done it before; the grief of Marcus over the outraged and mutilated Lavinia has dulled our sense of shock and nausea by the unavoidable appreciation of the beauty of the lines and their delivery, and here again, more simply, the mere assonance has kept us, *in performance,* from the revulsion or ridicule which the scene may arouse when we read it in the printed text.

He resolves the situation in perhaps the only possible way, by making the survivors let themslves go and make all the noise they can, while Lucius, Marcus and presumably the little boy, 'the poor remainder of Andronici', go up into the gallery over the stage and address the crowd from there.

At the sight of them the clamour has died down, and the words of Marcus come out with an impresive sonority. The very opening, 'You sad-faced men, people and sons of Rome' has the ring of the true Shakespearean music, and the theme is that which from the first scene of his first play has always brought out the best in him—the misery and downfall of a house divided against itself, and the hope that lies in the healing of old antagonisms and the avoidance of new ones. It was not 50 years since the death of Henry VIII and the troubles of succession; just 40 since the days of Mary Tudor and a king-consort who was also king of Spain. The older members of the audience would have keen memories of it all, and would understand the need for tolerance

> Lest Rome herself be bane unto herself,
> And she whom mighty kingdoms curtsey to,
> Like a forlorn and desperate castaway
> Do shameful execution on herself.

Unlike some of his characters, Shakespeare is not trying to stir up the emotions of an apathetic nation; the sentiment is one which he and his auditors all shared in common, and very well he knew it. The play was a success, and remained one long enough to arouse the resentment of Ben Jonson 20 years later, and provoke a disparaging allusion in the Induction to *Bartholomew Fair.*

Chapter Three

STARS IN CONJUNCTION

AFTER THE TROUBLE in June 1592, theatrical enterprise in London had rather a bad time. Just as the matter of the riot was blowing over, and theatres appeared likely to be available again, there was an outbreak of plague, with its consequent prohibition of miscellaneous assemblies. Companies could not hold together in London; they dissolved, re-formed, or amalgamated for provincial tours, and theatrical managements, under this patron or that, arose, appear for a little while in the scanty records and pass again into oblivion. The Lord Strange's Men were on the road; so were the Admiral's. Pembroke's had been, but by the summer of 1593 they were at a standstill, and had had to pawn their costumes. We have no evidence to show us what Shakespeare was doing just then to earn a living, but his two long poems of *Venus and Adonis* and *The Rape of Lucrece* were published in 1593 and 1594 respectively. Both were dedicated to Henry Wriothesley, Earl of Southampton, and show that Shakespeare had found a patron.

Patronage, in such a case, usually meant paying for something, but it appears from the number of editions that the books sold well, and Southampton would feel gratified at having encouraged a deserving writer. Rowe, in 1709, mentions an assertion that Southampton gave Shakespeare 'a thousand Pounds to enable him to go through with a Purchas which he heard he had a mind to', but it is evident that he found this rather hard to believe, since he says he would not have ventured to include it in his life of Shakespeare had he not been assured that it rested on the authority of Davenant—which, as has been indicated, is not enough for a good many later scholars. Chambers points out that Shakespeare's 'entire known purchases in real estate and

25

tithes throughout his life' did not run into four figures. He
suggests, very plausibly, that Southampton might have put
up £100 for Shakespeare to buy a share in the Lord
Chamberlain's company of players, which was formed
in 1594. If so, it was money well bestowed, not only for
the poet but, as it turned out, for his fellows and for succeeding generations, and there is one play, attributable to this
period and quite obviously written for private performance
in the smart, witty surroundings of a nobleman's household,
which may conceivably have brought poet, player and patron
into so harmonious an alliance that it gave occasion afterwards for this useful gift. That play is *Love's Labour's Lost*,
which is recorded as having been played before Elizabeth I
in 1597 and Anne of Denmark in 1605, but apparently did
not suit the taste of later, progressively-minded audiences.
Pepys does not mention it, nor does the exhaustive Genest;
a lady of blue-stocking inclinations, who bought the nine
volumes of Hanmer's pocket Shakespeare for a pound in
1759, stigmatized it as 'bad' in a marginal inscription, and
no performance of it is recorded between the Restoration
and the Vestris revival of it in 1839. Phelps put it on, shortly
afterwards, in his period of management at Sadlers Wells,
but it has had to wait until the present century to come
back into popular favour.

Originally, however, it was thought well worth reviving
for the entertainment of King James's consort in the early
days of 1605. A still-extant letter from Sir Walter Cope to
Robert Cecil, who was to be her host, is well known, but is
worth quoting here for the picture it gives of the anxieties
and preparations connected with a royal visit.

> I have sent and been all this morning hunting for
> players, jugglers and such kind of creature, but find
> them hard to find, wherefore leaving notes for them to
> seek me. Burbage is come, and says there is no new play
> that the queen hath not seen, but they have revived an
> old one, called Love's Labour's Lost, which for wit and
> mirth, he says, will please her exceedingly. And this is
> appointed to be played to-morrow night at my Lord
> Southampton's, unless you send a writ to remove the

corpus cum causa to your house in Strand. Burbage is my messenger attending your pleasure.

The question must have been serious indeed, for Burbage to be sent round with this letter to the nobleman who was in due course to become the famous Lord Salisbury, and on whom the king relied so much. The Revels Accounts indicate that *Love's Labour's Lost* was indeed performed by the King's Men, but they are vague about the date, putting it down merely as 'between New Year's Day and Twelfth Day'. We know from Dudley Carleton's correspondence that the queen and her *entourage* were feasted by Lord Southampton at about that time, and by Cecil two days later, so that we can understand, though not perhaps approve, Cope's discreditable suggestion that Cecil should arrange with Burbage to transfer the booking and secure the unfamiliar attraction for his own Royal Occasion. It is not recorded whether or not he succeeded in doing so, but he was both astute and unscrupulous, and the very fact of Cope's making the proposal suggests a strong likelihood that he might try.

This little sidelight on the play explains a great deal, because it shows us how players and patrons regarded it in its own day, and how we can advantageously try to regard it likewise. Burbage's recommendation of it suggests that he knew very well how effective it could be made, but we may permissibly assume that it was written to suit his particular talents. It is a piece of brilliant verbal chamber-music, much of it to be played at conversational pace, before an audience close enough to hear and sensitive enough to understand without the necessity for special emphasis, or for pauses to let this or that point sink in. The verbal exchanges are lighter even than the usual analogies of tennis or swordplay; the ideas fly from one to another not with the force of a fives-ball, but with the feathered lightness of a shuttlecock. It is a play about elegant and witty people of high station, and was now to be performed (and is most likely to have been originally written) for the diversion of people of high station who were—or liked to think they were—elegant and witty likewise. In those days it was the characters, and in a lesser degree the interpreters, who mattered, rather than the man who had invented them; Cope's letter speaks for the virtues and good sport of the play, but the writer sees no reason to mention that it was one of Shakespeare's. Perhaps he did not know, or it did not occur to him to ask. The author's name was not, at that time, a guarantee of quality; in later centuries it was an incubus, when 'Shakespeare' had become something to be approached and read with reverence. So approached, and imagined as being played in theatres of the size of Drury Lane, Covent Garden, or the Lyceum, it would seem to be intolerably dull. The large-theatre technique of the 18th and 19th centuries meant that Shakespeare had to be played rather slowly and very loudly, which does not suit this play at all. One can imagine that if Irving had played Berowne, and Ellen Terry either Rosaline or the Princess of France, in the Waterloo Chamber at Windsor for the delectation of Queen Victoria, the conversation in it might have sprung suddenly into life, but in less intimate conditions, and before the normal Lyceum audience, it would have failed of its effect and have done Shakespeare, Irving and his theatre a disservice thereby. It was really the revolution in the pace of Shakespearean speaking associated with Granville Barker and his productions early in the present century that made it possible to present the plays practically uncut, and brought *Love's Labour's Lost* to life as a practical possibility in the commercial theatre, for the sound, in this play alone, is even more important than the sense.

Like many a piece of symphonic music, it begins with a short introductory passage in slow time. The King of Navarre addresses his favoured courtiers in lines that have the ring of Marlowe, and once again Marlowe at his best. Matter and manner are blended with such art that there is none of the pomposity which is apt to occur in the earlier poet's work, and which Shakespeare unerringly parodied in the conversation of Ancient Pistol. Instead of obvious rhetoric, there is poetry; instead of orotundity there is a note of grave earnestness that puts forward the King's proposal in the best possible light, and makes one believe, for the first few minutes, that it is a reasonable one, partly because the speech does not go into details. It is clear that the plan involves some kind of training, for life rather than for any particular sport, and what stands out is the excellence of the motive—that cultivation of the art of living, by the subjugation and control of personal desires, that shall make the court of Navarre in three years' time the wonder of the world—but the speech is concerned with enunciating the principle, not specifying the practice. It ends with a rhymed couplet that gives an air of finality to the whole, and makes a fit accompaniment to the King's signature when he appends it to the formal articles of association. Longaville and Dumaine in turn accompany their signatures with quatrains of easy approval, each of them ending in a couplet, and then comes the turn of the gay but practical Berowne. At once the music of high ideals is enlivened by a cheerful little tune of common-sense, always respectful and in key with what has gone before, but resolute to go into all the details and embroider the absurdities. The desire to read what one is signing, and to know exactly what one is letting oneself in for, is just as natural in our day as it was in Shakespeare's, and the expression of it is just as unwelcome to those who have already signed a pledge without carefully considering its implications.

Naturally enough, Berowne's attitude is highly disconcerting to the King, who devised the scheme, and to his fellow-courtiers who took it up so readily and so rashly. They remonstrate with him in a scene in which earnestness and good-humour are made unfamiliar yoke-fellows to carry it lightly along. In regard to sense, we have the regular thrust and parry of argument, either side being stoutly and intelligently maintained, but the sound of the words contrives to keep the conversation pleasant, and lets the contestants disagree without being disagreeable. The use of strict verse-form is largely responsible for this. As in a good fencing-match the combatants, with all their speed and ingenuity, are careful to maintain their style and not let the encounter degenerate into scuffling, so here. Flat contradiction is delivered in the most courteous manner possible. An argument is put forward and opposed, but the opposition is couched in words that balance the argument in form and agree with it in rhyme. It is artificial, but that very artificiality is a matter of courtesy and compliment, as it implies consideration for other people, and presents the most stubborn opposition with scrupulous care to avoid giving offence.

It is with something like an apologetic tone that Berowne produces his trump card—the fact that in swearing to shun the company of womankind for three years, the King has forgotten that the Princess of France is expected shortly on an official diplomatic mission. In the circumstances, the King rules that 'on mere necessity' the strict letter of the experiment must be dispensed with, and that is enough for Berowne. Once that word 'necessity' has been admitted as a saving clause, he accepts it as available on other occasions when required, so he makes no more ado, but signs the pledge in what a later writer, well versed in the degrees of human frailty and fallibility, was to describe as 'a Pickwickian sense'.

At the same time, he asks if there is not to be anything in the way of light relief to their course of study, and the King's answer introduces a further variation in the verse-form. It is a characteristic Shakespearean sonnet in all essentials but one, since its three quatrains are followed by a triple rhyme instead of the ordinary couplet. Even so, in actual delivery it may be—and quite possibly should be—spoken with a full stop at the end of the penultimate line, letting this round off the sonnet in the usual way, the third rhyme coming after it like an echo and a summing-up, even as the first line of the speech has echoed the last word of Berowne's enquiry.

So much for form; in subject it has other resemblances, being itself an epigram, rather like those written by John Davies of Hereford in the style of Martial, in which the poet summarises and satirises the characteristics, and usually the shortcomings, of well-known people. There have been so many attempts to identify characters in this day with familiar figures in the Elizabethan world that there has been a later and very natural reaction against anything of the sort, but in this instance there are one or two points about the speech that are worth consideration.

For one thing, it arbitrarily introduces a new character, of whom we have not heard and for whom we have not been prepared, and goes on to describe him in considerable detail; He is a 'refined traveller of Spain', full of the latest fashions of verbal extravagance and immoderately pleased with his own fantastication. At the same time, he is 'a man of complements' with undeniably good qualities to balance his absurdities, so that good and ill in him are pretty evenly matched, and he is full of stories of old times and heroes who have been forgotten in the later course of the world's history. All this may be taken as a 'build-up' for the entry of a leading actor, but there seems every likelihood that it would be accepted, by an audience of Elizabethan courtiers, as a brilliant and unflattering portrait of someone whom everybody knew and nobody very greatly liked.

Sir Walter Ralegh's name has been suggested. Southampton did not like him at all, and Southampton's friend Essex was his implacable enemy. His portrait shows that, provincial or no, he was possessed of that grave dignity that was at its height in the nobility of Spain, and whether or not Shakespeare intended Don Adriano de Armado to be a caricature of him, Elizabethan playgoers of Southampton's faction might well be excused for thinking that he did. The very manner of his presentation in the King's speech, as someone admitted into that noble, learned company as a butt, might be taken as a welcome explanation for Ralegh's unquestionable, unpardonable success in the Court circles which meant so much to them, and his infatuation with Jacquenetta the 'day-woman' could echo Ralegh's courtship and matrimonial arrangements, which, if John Aubrey is to be believed, were the subject of a cheerful and unrefined story in their own day.

All the same, it would be unwise to accept Don Adriano wholeheartedly as a likeness of any individual. He is a study of an easily-imagined type, and in 10 years' time just such another figure, lean, fantastic in appearance and filled with illusions and extravagances inspired by a long study of inferior fiction, was to be let loose upon the literature of the western world. Don Adriano de Armado and Don Quixote de la Mancha would have understood each other had

it been their fortune to meet, and may be imagined exchanging salutations of grave absurdity and passing on their several
ways fully satisfied, without the need of a formal encounter
in arms.

After all this preparation, the audience might expect to
see the fantastic foreigner at once, but Shakespeare is more
ingenious than that. He brings in a letter from him, introduced by two of the clowns, and rhyme and rhythm are
abandoned for very colloquial dialogue. The clowns are
contrasted in the usual manner for such 'double acts' in
Shakespeare or anywhere else, one of them being very
stupid and the other very cheerful and loquacious. Master
Dull, the constable, is out of his depth at once. After saying
who he is, he finds the explanation of his errand quite
beyond him, and leaves it to the letter, and to his prisoner
Costard, to explain the position, himself lapsing into silence
except for a moment of consciousness at the sound of his
own name. Costard, on the other hand, is ready to do the
talking for both, and to interrupt the reading of the letter
with interjections, explanations and corroborations lightly
thrown in as a seasoning to the main text. It is only when
the King and his two friends have taken their leave, and
Costard has been marched off under the guardianship of
the witty Berowne and the inarticulate Constable Dull, that
the word-music returns to the high fantastic style again, not
this time in metre, but in the extravagance of Euphuistic
prose.

Now at last we see the fantastical Spaniard, full of elegant
and exaggerated expressions in his conversation, and instinctively attitudinising and playing to an audience, even if that
audience is no one but his own diminutive page, who is more
than a match for him in respectful but acute comment.
Armado's conversation may be cited in support of the
theory that the play was written for private performance to
a small audience at close range. Spoken conversationally,
with no more slowing-down than the actual enunciation
requires, it is an entertaining performance by someone who
is a blend of the wit, the professor and the *poseur*; but in
a large theatre, with the rallendando necessary to make
every word carry to the far back of the house, it calls for

drastic cutting, or it loses its tension, like a sagging tennis-net, and Armado becomes a bore. As with the cheerful trivialities of Romeo's conversation with Mercutio, lightness is all.

The entry of the Princess, with her three ladies and their attendant Boyet, brings us back to regular blank verse of considerable charm, in which explanation is combined with ornament, and in the course of the scene we are given not only character-sketches of the King's three young companions, but a shrewd indication of what the Princess's three ladies think of them. When the King comes out to bid them welcome, he is instantly at a disadvantage because he cannot offer them the hospitality of the court, and the Princess loses no time in seizing the opportunity, catching up word after word and throwing each lightly back to him in gentle but quite unrelenting raillery. Once again the echo of the same word, bandied about from voice to voice, lends to the situation a kind of dancing music, and prepares the way for a sudden change, when the Princess produces the written statement of her mission, and the music subsides as the King studies the document in silence.

For at this point, one may say, the silence *is* the music. We have come to the first moment of real, serious tension in the play, to what Thomas Danett, in his Elizabethan translation of Philip de Commines, calls 'an interview between two great princes for treaty of their affairs', and that tension affects practically everyone on the stage. The King of Navarre is intent upon the letter, the Princess of France is intent upon the King, and the lords and ladies around are intent upon both of them. Like the great pedal-point E flat that underlies the opening minutes of *Das Rheingold*, the silence grows and grows until it is hardly to be borne, and is varied, rather than broken, by Berowne in an exchange of whispered trivialities with the masked lady nearest to him. There is nothing deliberately intriguing or provocative about the mask; it is as much a matter of ordinary dress as the shady hat and hatpin-fastened veil that some of us can still remember as the outdoor habit of our Edwardian elders, and the very fact that the ladies were all wearing their travelling-masks would help to remind the audience that the interview, more appropriate to the Presence Chamber and cloth of state, was being conducted in the open air.

The tension is resolved, for the present, by the King's summary of the differences between them and the disclosure, by Boyet, that the vital piece of evidence, the packet with the receipts for the money in dispute, has not in fact arrived, though it is hourly expected. The King accepts the position, defers further argument until the evidence is available, and withdraws. Once again the use of a rhyming couplet marks the end of an episode, like a full close in music, and the tempo changes to one of brisk informality. Masks and polite restrictions are alike laid aside, and Berowne and Rosaline are free to continue their badinage in the light, lilting measure of a dance. When his companions in their turn question Boyet about the ladies who have attracted them, the rhythm becomes that of a lively jig, with the general cadence of the nursery rhyme beginning

> There was an old woman, and what do you think?
> She lived upon nothing but victuals and drink,

but admitting a free use of extra, patterning syllables as found, for instance, in the popular Victorian ditty of Villikins and his Dinah. This note of high spirits continues to the end of the scene. Even the elderly Boyet roundly diagnoses Navarre's feelings for the princess, who is unable to deny it, but hastily changes the subject by calling the ladies to attend her to the 'pavilion' which is their head-quarters in the park. With a final round of rhyming disrespect for the old gentleman they go on their way, with Boyet chuckling after them.

The Princess and Rosaline have had most of the witty replies, Maria coming as a fair third, but Katharine has had practically nothing. The company could not be expected to have an infinity of intelligent boy-players to draw upon, and one of them is wanted for the men's side of the encounter, in the shape of Moth, the Spaniard's 'little nimble page', whose pert, worldly-wise comments are now brought in to offset and satirise his master's aestheticisms, and incidentally to vary the performance with a song. His precocious court-wit makes a contrast, as does his smart appearance, to the shrewd country-wit of Costard the clown, and to the drawling affectation of Armado, whose manner with subordinates is rather that of the Victorian 'swell', like Lord Dundreary in *Our American Cousin*, or the refined and superior being, like the rival poets in *Patience*. Elizabethan humour—and particularly Shakespearean humour—was not always so very different from our own. The joke about the Envoy and the Goose is admittedly obscure, and may refer to some contemporary personality, or some forgotten children's game on the lines of 'Adam and Eve and Pinch-me', by which the innocent victim was led to pronounce a formula that identified him with the goose. The speaking of the *envoi* to a ballade, for instance, might be accompanied by a traditional advance, flourish or salutation that Moth would not perform on giving the mere words of the couplet, but which Armado would consider appropriate to an *Envoi*. His delivery of the absurd lines, accompanied by that ceremonial flourish, would then carry some suggestion of the deep bow, stoop and wriggle with which a goose goes under a gate and straightens itself up afterwards. This is no more than conjecture, but may serve to indicate one way in which the sound of the text might make sense, or at least intelligible nonsense, when accompanied by appropriate action.

Other things, like the over-economical tip that is given with a long name and a grand gesure, are as fresh to-day as they were in Shakespeare's. The remuneration that is 'the Latin word for three farthings' is soon succeeded by Berowne's 'guerdon' of a shilling, and as Costard goes off, highly gratified, on his new errand, the true music returns again. The cynical, lighthearted, bantering Berowne is in love, is too honest not to admit it, and at the same time too consistent not to assail it with the ridicule that he would—and very soon does—apply to any of his friends in the same unhappy condition. For the first time we are looking more deeply into the man's tormented mind, and seeing at the same time how the frank admission and recognition of one's feelings can make them bearable, and that self-mockery, when honestly carried out, can leave little room for the

baser emotion of self-pity. All of a sudden the play has
become momentarily serious, and done something to show
us what its title means.

With the opening of the fourth act, we are at once given,
in two lines, the sense of movement, energy and enjoyment
of the open air. It is all so natural that we have no time to
appreciate how well it is done. Those words

> Was that the King that spurred his horse so hard
> Against the steep uprising of the hill?

show us at once where the Princess and her ladies are, while
the bows they carry, and the presence of the attendant
forester, indicate what they are about to do. In the next
line, Boyet's uncertainty suggests that they are all looking
at someone in the far distance, and in that which follows
we can see that he is now out of sight, and the Princess is
ready to turn to other things. The official mission is suspended until the messenger with the receipt and other papers
arrives from France, and the interim may be spent in sport,
compliments and light philosophising. With the entry of the
clown Costard, the metre changes to that of Villikins and
his Dinah once more, with the Spaniard's letter to the dairy-
maid forming an interlude of elaborate and affected prose.
When the Princess goes off to her butt, with the foresters
in attendance, her ladies and Boyet linger for a few minutes
in conversation that still preserves the jigging metre but
contrives to blend a surface-elegance of phrase with an
incredible amount of underlying obscenity. Little by little
the group disperses, leaving Costard alone, full of congratu-
lation for his own wit and ready to dismiss the courtly Boyet
(whose contributions have been as indecent as anybody's)
as 'a most simple clown', till the shouts 'within' tell him that
the deer is started, the hunt is up, and he runs whooping
away to see it, so that the scene ends in the key of its
beginning.

Learned absurdity returns in the next interlude, but to
a different tune. Instead of the elaboration of the aesthete,
grounded on an almost pathological desire to express the
finest, most delicate *nuances* of his meaning, we have the dogmatic arrogance of the pedant, bringing out his unquestioned

scholarship for his own self-glorification and the satisfaction of impressing or contradicting other people. Holofernes the schoolmaster may be learned, but he is not lovable, and our sympathies go more readily with Sir Nathaniel the curate—equally learned, perhaps, but no match for him in self-esteem—or even the slow-witted constable Dull, who tries manfully to follow their conversation by making a contribution of his own in the shape of a countryman's riddle which falls completely flat, because the scholars both know the answer, though Sir Nathaniel gives it in a word beyond the constable's understanding. Here prose is varied by snatches of the now familiar ballad-rhythms, but they come out with a kind of polysyllabic twittering on the lips of the curate and contrast with the steam-roller orotundity of the schoolmaster. When the illiterate Jacquenetta brings in a love-letter and asks the parson to read it for her, the schoolmaster is instantly piqued at being passed over, and rumbles away in assumed indifference, breaking into Latin and Italian and even humming up the scale, until he can restrain his curiosity no longer and has to ask roundly what is in the letter, and crane over to look at it and find that it is in verse.

When Sir Nathaniel obligingly reads it aloud, it is revealed as a true Shakespearean sonnet, though Holofernes hastens to find fault both with the reading and with the lines themselves. It is not, after all, Don Adriano's letter to Jacquenetta —which Costard has already handed in error to the Princess— but Berowne's to Rosaline, and Costard has ill-earned his shilling guerdon and three-farthing remuneration by getting the letters mixed. This little episode, and the pedant's injunction to bring the letter to the notice of the King, combine to link the scene with the main plot, such as it is, and give it some pretext for being there at all, apart from that of providing space for a 'turn' by a different pair of comedians.

After this little exercise in satiric comedy there comes an unexpected change of style. The concert of verbal chamber-music suddenly becomes a play; the scene not only involves brilliant conversation, as before, but a dramatic situation as well. For the first time something actually *happens,* and happens on the stage, and the situation is intensified by what the audience see, as well as by what they hear. And, moreover, what they have seen and heard is seen to have its influence in turn on the characters themselves, inducing a change of mind, so that their purpose at the end of the scene is diametrically opposite to what it had been at the beginning, not only of the scene but of the whole play. And, for the first time, it is made clear that the leading figure is quite unquestionably Berowne. Hitherto he has been notable as odd-man-out, the shrewd, critical commentator on the project of scholarly celibacy, but now he is revealed as truly one with his fellows, embarrassed by love as deeply as any of them, and in his capitulation, and admission of it, he is accepted instinctively as the leader of them all.

When he comes in, he is seen to be driven yet one stage nearer to frenzy by his unsought, unquestionable, irresistible passion. When it first caught him, he was instinctively able to make it tolerable by mocking it, and mocking himself for feeling it; now the matter has gone past mockery, past poetry, and he is tormenting himself in prose. There is something familiar, too, about the style and cadence of the prose, and the vehemence of its expression. We have heard it before, and laughed at it, in the elaborate epistles of Don Adriano de Armado. Berowne himself has summarised it as 'not the best that I looked for, but the best that ever I heard' when the Spaniard's affectations were paraded for us before he himself put in an appearance, and since then, in the letter wrongly delivered to the Princess and her ladies, we have seen how that fantastic gentleman expresses himself in love. And now here is Berowne, the self-sufficient, cynical Berowne, undergoing the same perplexities and expressing himself in the same extravagant way, with puns, antitheses, self-accusation, self-contradiction, self-torment and self-contempt. At the very outset there is something deeper even than that. 'They have pitched a toil', he says of the King and his huntsmen; 'I am toiling in a pitch—pitch that defiles.' He has already made, in his earlier comments, a most unflattering account of his Rosaline, her personal appearance and her probable morals, and he knows that this realisation makes no difference to the purely animal passion that is rising within him. Here, if anywhere, is Shakespeare's dramatisation of those terrible sonnets 129 and its successor, be they bred of experience or tormented imagination. The only mitigation of the agony is the hope—admittedly an unworthy one—that other people are suffering in the same way, and it is with a feeling of relief that Berowne retires into concealment as the King comes in with a paper in his hand.

It is a sobering thought, after all the solemn dogmatism and shrill contradiction that has been written about the Sonnets, to reflect that Shakespeare could, and did, use the form effectively and dramatically in a light comedy when he thought fit. The first 14 lines of the King's love-message might well find a place in the sequence—say, as a preliminary to Sonnet 74—and the extra couplet added at the end is the only link, by its mention of a royal recipient, between the poem and its avowed purpose in the play. Even so, we cannot be quite sure that the couplet appeared at all in the original version; the earliest known edition of the play is the 1598 quarto, which proclaims it on its title-page to be 'As it was presented before her Highness this last Christmas', and the complimentary couplet is just the sort of thing that might have been slipped in as appropriate to the royal occasion. Without it, the text still makes sense, the theme of grief with which the sonnet concludes being echoed in the King's words as he drops the paper among the leaves.

When Longaville appears in a few moments' time, the poet is ready with another one, which once more betokens its author in beauty of sound and ingenuity of argument. Dumaine produces something in a different metre, that of *A Lover's Complaint*, but once again it has the true Shakespearean ring. On the stage, it is the existence of the verses, and the cumulative effect of courtier after courtier turning poet, that is amusing; studied on the printed page (which is unfair, as the play was meant to be seen and heard, not read) they give the impression that the lovers have felt incapable of producing their own lyrics and have secretly and independently engaged one William Shakespeare to write something to serve their turn.

In their various places of concealment, the King mocks
Longaville, he and Longaville mock Dumaine, and Berowne
at last emerges radiant with mockery of them all, until he
sees Costard and Jacquenetta coming along with a letter
that he recognises as his own. He breaks off abruptly and
tries to hurry away, but the King stops him, and in a few
minutes Berowne is revealed to be as lovesick as the rest
of them. He is, as ever, the quickest-witted of them all, and
the readiest to accept the situation and turn it to advantage.
In the lilting, jig-metre of a dance he agrees soundly that
'You three fools lacked *me* fool to make up the mess', and
unconsciously suggests the clowns' obscure nursery-rhyme
about the goose whose entry 'squared the odds by adding
four'. No sooner have Costard and Jacquenetta taken themselves off than he bursts out into a lyrical greeing of his
fellow-lovers, welcoming their passion and proclaiming the
beauty of his dark-haired Rosaline against the fairest lady
any of them can champion. The arguments of the contestants
are set forth in sestet, couplet or quatrain, and the poetry
pours out of them all in a wonderful ensemble—particularly,
one may imagine, in the intimacy of a chamber performance,
where there is no need to strain the voice by speaking above
conversation-pitch. Vocal inflections can impress by their
quiet sincerity as we listen to four lovers uttering the poetry
of love.

This cannot last, however. The King calls the others to
'leave this chat', and urges Berowne to find some argument
to justify their change of views and keep them free from
the charge of oath-breaking. Longaville asks for 'authority'
and the practical Dumaine flatly wants 'some salve for
perjury'. Berowne responds to the challenge with a ringing
speech of exhortation, at once a glorification of love in
general and a confirmation of his original claim that their
vows of abstinence were unreasonable and unnatural. It is a
summons to them all to appear in the lists and break a lance
for Love, and the King's reaction is very like a battle-cry
from one of the Histories, but invoking St. Cupid instead
of St. George. Berowne in his answer keeps up the metaphor
of battle, but Longaville calls them to 'lay these glozes by'
and get on with the business of wooing. The King agrees,

and the act ends with their eager determination to arrange
appropriate entertainments and make up for lost time. The
high pretensions of their original enterprise (which may well
have sprung from nothing more inspiring than boredom)
are not exactly thrown overboard, but are relegated to
the background, to give place to more interesting and
important things.

Quite apart from its dramatic and literary merits, the
whole scene is worth considering for the pointers it gives
to the likeliest date and place of its first performance, which
Quiller-Couch and Dover Wilson assigned to the Christmas
festivities of 1593 at 'some great private house, possibly
the Earl of Southampton's'. As we have seen, the play shows
the King of Navarre deciding to abandon his original
programme of stern asceticism for a good and sufficient
reason, and Berowne, Longaville and Dumaine doing the
same beside him. Now in December 1593 the title King of
Navarre meant to most Londoners just what it means to those
of us who were stirred in our youth with the romances of
Stanley Weyman and the elder Dumas. Henri de Bourbon,
son of Jeanne d'Albret, Queen of Navarre, had risen from
being the orphan ruler of an insignificant and poverty-
stricken little kingdom in the Pyrenees to be the champion
of the Huguenots in the Wars of Religion, the victor of
Arques and Ivry, and now, by the death and at the nomination of Henri III, last of the house of Valois, had been
proclaimed king of France under the name of Henri IV.
When Boyet, at his own first entrance, spoke of

> the sole inheritor
> Of all perfections that a man may owe,
> Matchless Navarre,

that name would suggest one man above all to an English
audience. Many gentlemen had known him personally, and
had fought beside him or under him in his struggle to take
up his inheritance; only two years before, in November
1591, the Earl of Essex, at the head of an English force of
7,000 men, had helped to capture Rouen from the still-
resisting powers of the Holy League, and playgoers in
general had seen him depicted on the stage still more

recently in Marlowe's *Tragedy of the Guise,* subsequently published as *The Massacre at Paris.* In addition to his historical importance and military reputation, he was widely known as the enthusiastic and indiscreet pursuer of a succession of attractive ladies (a taste inherited in due course by his English grandson, King Charles II), one of his generals was the Duc de Longueville, his marriage with a princess of France (which led to his narrowly escaping death in the Massacre of St. Bartholomew's Eve) had been arranged through the mediation of the elder Marshal Biron, the younger Biron was one of his closest friends, and the last of his Catholic enemies, as yet unreconciled, was the fat Duc de Mayenne, brother of the Duc de Guise, and presented in Marlowe's play as the implacable and murderous Dumaine.

All four names, then, had strong associations for courtly and theatre-going Elizabethans, particularly at this point in the play, when the gentlemen concerned abandon their programme of intensive study for the more serious business of love-making. In spite of Henri's nomination by his dying predecessor, in spite of his military success and his welcome so widely expressed over the greater part of France, there were still strongholds of Catholicism that implacably held out against him, and the greatest of these was Paris itself. Until he was accepted there, he was powerless to do the thing that was most important in his eyes, namely to administer a peaceful and united France, and bring her back to prosperity. He had stood up unflinchingly for his Huguenot faith while it was undergoing danger and persecution; now it had gained its freedom and could be established in that freedom by a royal decree. His interests were all for tolerance rather than for uncompromising dogmatism, and in the cause of that tolerance, after months of deliberation and discussion, he made formal application, in July 1593, to be received into the Church of Rome.

Elizabeth of England was shocked, apprehensive and distressed, and wrote him a letter of protest and regret, showing how gravely he had disappointed her, but it must have been quite soon apparent that there was to be no realisation of her worst fears. The king's action did not imply peace with Spain, with the danger to England that such a peace would carry with it, and very soon Elizabeth was writing to him with her old familiarity, and signing herself 'Your affectionate sister and cousin' as before. Meanwhile, there is no evidence that her alarm had been shared by everyone. To Southampton in particular, whose family had a Catholic background, the advantages of the change could be made more easily apparent than to Elizabeth, who had her own personal remembrances of danger and tribulation which Southampton was too young to have known. If it was for him, and not for the Court, that the play was written, then the argument of Berowne would have 'no offence in't', and might be taken as an amusing and slightly daring comment on the course of public affairs.

Significant in this connection, too, is the allusion, on the title-page already mentioned to the fact that this 'pleasant conceited comedy' had been played before the Queen the previous Christmas. By Christmas 1597 the threatened Spanish intervention had been crushed—with English aid—by the recovery of Amiens in September, after a campaign which the new king had practically opened with his announcement that he had 'long enough played the King of France, and it was high time he played the King of Navarre'. He had gone back to his old campaigning days and been successful. Shakespeare's play about a King of Navarre was once more topical and this time unexceptionable, and it was safe to let the Queen see it. If any additional precaution were considered necessary, it could be provided by giving him the name of Ferdinand in the printed stage-direction, as an equivalent to the modern announcement, at the beginning of some novels, that 'no reference is intended to any living person'. The name was there in print, but nowhere in the spoken text, and if audiences instinctively identified 'matchless Navarre' with a distinguished contemporary, that was their responsibility alone. No one could say that players or playwright had told them to do so.

If, then, we follow Quiller-Couch and Dover Wilson and date the play to December 1593, a good many other things fall nearly into place, explaining themselves and each other. Henslowe's season on the South Bank had come to a sudden and very definite stop. The actors were at a loose end, and while some of them went on tour, or to other companies (incidentally taking with them their own garbled versions of *King Henry VI*), Shakespeare had recently earned some public notice for himself, and commendation for his patron Southampton, by publishing a very successful, though to some minds a not very proper, poem on a classical subject. The author of *Venus and Adonis* was someone worth encouragement and, if necessary, a certain amount of practical help. His playhouse background need not necessarily be a disadvantage; he might be commissioned to write a play in the lyrical style that had already brought him to favourable notice, and a private performance of it would be an interesting and original form of entertainment for his patron's friends. As for the actors, those most likely to be available were those tied, by family or other connections, to Burbage's original Theatre. Companies centred round a management could go out on the road when plague or the magistrates made London impossible; a company centred round an actual building, its own property, would have to stay at home, or leave somebody at home, 'to mind the shop'. In this combination of circumstances, there is a case for concluding that the first play Shakespeare wrote 'out of his own head: was *Love's Labour's Lost,* and that the first part he wrote specially and deliberately for Richard Burbage was Berowne.

It is a part well suited to the versatility that we know to have been Burbage's particular charateristic. He has to be, in succession, the shrewd, dry commentator on other men's ideas, the smart society conversationalist, the serious, self-confessed, self-critising, reluctantly self-tormenting lover, and finally the champion of love, producing arguments of ingenious, defiant causistry for the justification of 'affection's men-at-arms'. It is a real *tour de force*, and not all Berownes are able to rise up to it, but it is quite obvious that somebody, almost certainly Burbage, *was,* and a success in the part would show both author and actor that each had taken the other's measure, and that they might work together, for mutual pleasure and profit, on the professional stage. Here, also, is good cause and occasion for that gesture of Southampton's which Chambers has suggested as being the purchase, for Shakespeare, of a share in the company of the Chamberlain's Men. He was putting up the capital to establish a partnership that would last for years, and would earn him, in the succeeding centuries, more gratitude than he, or even the immediate beneficiaries, could possibly have imagined.

Their great resolve once taken, the lords woo the ladies in every way they can think of. First they send gifts, which the ladies receive, compare and comment on in rhyme; then they arrive in the conventional masque-form as exotic visitors coming to pay their respects to beauty; but the ladies have been forwarned by Boyet, and are more than a match for them, assuming masks in their turn and exchanging the presents they have just received, so that each nobleman, tracking down his gift and pursuing its owner, pledges himself passionately to the wrong lady. Once again the rhymed couplet helps to give the effect of smart, courtly conversation, simply because it instinctively suggests a quickness of uptake and the instant ability to cap each remark with an answer in its own key. The 'Muscovites' retire worsted, return again in their own persons and are involved in further confusion till Berowne diagnoses the trick and denounces Boyet—without naming him—as the eavesdropper who betrayed them. Hard upon this comes the entry of the comic characters with their Masque of the Nine Worthies, who speak in ballad metre. Costard the clown, as Pompey, acquits himself well, but the curate has stage-fright, and is removed in confusion, the page, as the Infant Hercules, is given nothing to say, Holofernes the pedant loses his temper with a critic in the audience and is hooted off the field, and Don Adriano, as Hector, has survived the courtiers' comments when he gets involved in a quarrel with Pompey, which is in its turn interrupted by the arrival of a messenger from France with the sudden, tragic news that the king of France is dead.

This totally unexpected ending must have come as a shock to the nobles in the audience as well as to those upon the stage. Berowne hints to the Worthies that they had better withdraw, and here again we see how much better suited the play is to a small, intimate auditorium than to a large theatre. Spoken too loudly, or too slowly, his line is intrusive, and sounds like a word of command given by someone without the authority to do so; but if it comes in little more than an undertone, but very promptly on its cue, it suggests a piece of good-natured advice from a man of quicker perception than the rest, and of ready consideration, now and then, for the feelings of other people. The comedians gratefully taken advantage of it, and the Spaniard covers their retreat with a few words of reassurance to Berowne—and to us—indicating that seedy and stilted as he is, without a shirt to his back, he knows what is due from him as a soldier and a gentleman. The hint, and the acknowledgement, give us in their quiet way a better view of the best side of Berowne.

In a few moments we see that he needs it. When the King's plea for serious consideration has proved too complicated and courtly for the Princess to take it in, he becomes the spokesman for his master and his fellow-lords of Navarre, in a speech of 'honest plain words' with neither rhymes nor witty 'conceits' in it, but this, too, is unavailing. The King has already granted the Princess what she originally came for, and she has formally thanked him. Now it is his turn to ask, and she has to admit that while listening to his and his friends' words of adoration, she and her ladies did not take them seriously. Dumaine and Longaville, in only a line and a half between them plead their cause more effectively than they had done with all their eloquence, and the ladies relent to the extent of agreeing to give the matter further consideration in a year's time, when the Court is out of mourning.

So the play draws to an end as it began, but with a difference. The King is once more committed to a period of self-denial and austerity, but this time he must be really alone, not enlivened with like-minded companions in a reading-party that may develop into a mutual admiration society. Dumaine and Longaville are told to go away and grow up, and Berowne's probation is to visit the sick and see if he can put his over-ready wit to better use, and succeed in giving pleasure to people who have little enough in life to laugh about. For a moment the idea disconcerts and shocks him, just as it may have come to the original courtly audience as a surprise, and not perhaps an immediately acceptable one, but the truth of Rosaline's contention and the promise it holds out to him are not to be ignored. He recovers his spirits, and accepts the commission with a smile and a rhyme for his lady and a wry admission to the King that their affairs cannot be wound up with a conventional happy ending before curtain-fall.

In this little episode Shakespeare has spoken, perhaps, more profoundly than he knew. For the first time he has put forth the idea that it is a natural and necessary quality of the great to recognise the difficulties of those who are less fortunate, and do what they can to help them. It is a doctrine that he puts most effectively into the mouths not of protesting figures like Jack Cade and Caliban, but of persons speaking with authority. Portia's speech on mercy is largely devoted to pointing out that that quality is a characteristic of greatness, the Duke of Vienna seeks to gain a better knowledge of his people by going among them in disguise, and perhaps the most poignant of all is the bitter cry of self-reproach at his own shortcomings, 'O, I have ta'en too little care of this', that bursts, on the threshold of madness, from the racked heart of Lear. It is a moment in which this early comedy and that late, tremendous tragedy join hand in hand.

But this is no note on which to end an evening of bright conversation among kindly, happy people. The rhythms of musical diction are made to give way to music itself as the Spaniard, shabby-genteel though he may be, comes forward in his unquestioned gentility to be the ambassador of the comic characters and to beg leave to present the song that was to end the masque. Boys' and men's voices sing their antiphons of spring and winter, and after that, there is no need for anything more. The words of Mercury himself, the god of eloquence, would come as an anticlimax after the singing, and with that brief admission the fantastical Spaniard politely dismisses the audience and bows his company away. The play is over, Lord Southampton's guests may disperse to other pursuits, and Shakespeare and Burbage, author and interpreter, may each have felt that he has found a colleague whom he would do well to cultivate. If time, place and function are what other scholars have suggested for them, we may justifiably assume that it was on this occasion, and with this play, that the great partnership began.

Chapter Four

THE NEW ENTERPRISE

THE TWO MEN were more than script-writer and player;
they were soon colleagues in a well-dowered theatrical
enterprise, and were to remain so for all their lives. By the
end of 1594, Shakespeare's name was associated with those
of Burbage and of William Kempe the comedian as
'servants to the Lord Chamberlain', and when the company
broke with the ground landlord of their original playhouse
and took a lease, in 1599, of the ground in Southwark, on
which to re-erect the transported timbers of the Theatre,
Richard and his brother Cuthbert shared half the enterprise
between them, the other half being borne by Shakespeare,
Kempe and three of their colleagues. It was a syndicate,
in which the Burbages held a controlling interest, since they
owned the fabric of the building itself, in addition to half
the shares in the land it stood on. Quite apart from his
unquestionable talent, it is clear to see who would be the
leading actor in that company, now established in the
building that was to become famous, through succeeding
centuries, as the Globe.

It was a great—practically an unbeatable—combination.
Henslowe had theatres of his own, he had in Alleyn a leading
player on whom he could rely, but he had not that extra
advantage of numbering among his actors a resident playwright who could provide suitable pieces as required, and
was always available at rehearsal. The official literary men,
the 'University wits', were often renowned as poets, but
were apt to be quarrelsome and unreliable, and not always
very honest. (Robert Greene, for instance, had been known
to sell the same play to two different managements.) The
Chamberlain's Men, on the other hand, had the Burbages,
the Burbage theatres, and William Shakespeare. They could,

and did, perform plays by other writers, but Shakespeare was always on the spot, to help them out of a difficulty, as when the Queen commanded a play about Falstaff in in love just when Kempe, their inimitable Falstaff, had left the company. How they got over that difficulty has been suggested elsewhere, but the important point is that they did so, and that Shakespeare's ingenuity was equal to the occasion.

At this stage we may do well to consider the first Shakespearean part in which Burbage gained really wide and long-enduring commendation. Ben Jonson, once the great Camden's pupil at Westminster, was notoriously patronising about Shakespeare's knowledge of the classics, but even 'small Latin and less Greek' is more than none at all, and implies at least a nodding acquaintance with the fact that classical authors had existed, and had written well, and been considered worth reading and discussing by people better qualified to do so. We simply do not know what he talked about, or listened to, in such leisure moments as he had, in tiring-house or tavern. A pot-companion with a classical background, like John Heywood, was capable of holding forth on any subject, when the mood took him, to anyone who would listen to him, and Shakespeare was just the man to benefit by such oddments of knowledge as might supplement what he knew already. He may or may not have known that it was the practice of the Greek tragedians to follow up a set of three serious dramas by something lighter, or he may have thought it, independently, a suitable course to follow. Be that as it may, he wrote a sequel to his three plays about Henry VI, and that sequel was in a very different vein. The star part in *Richard III* is one for an artist who can be tyrant, conspirator and, alternatively or at the same time, a sardonic comedian. The bloodthirsty chronicle of battle and intrigue in France and England, culminating in the murder of an imprisoned king, is rounded off by a kind of sinister harlequinade.

Bernard Shaw compared the play to the story of Punch and Judy, and the comparison is facile but, if too closely followed, misleading. Pursued in production, as it very often is, it does rather less than justice to the play and, it may be suggested, to the principal player, because the repeated advances in the manner of Punch, with its com- bination of carneying approach, savage violence and unctuous, chuckling hypocrisy, is apt to pall and give the impression of tedium, and of bad construction by the dramatist. One can get tired of the sidelong glance at the audience and the continuous air of 'See how well I'm doing this' that Shaw has compared to that of a Houndsditch sales- man cheating a factory girl over a pair of second-hand stockings.[1] We may get a different impression, however, by considering some of the actual words of the part, in the light of what we know about the people by whom, and for whom, it was created.

It is a great advantage to a dramatist if, while telling a story which is broadly familiar to his audience, he can interest and surprise them at the same time by showing that it has even more interest, variety and significance than they had supposed. One way of doing it is to contradict preconceived opinions, to represent one's villain as a misunderstood innocent, and one's hero as an insensitive and noisy egoist. This is quite useful when it is new, as it suggests originality, but when the newness has worn off it is apt to pall, and runs the risk of becoming a predictable characteristic of the playwright. It has to be very well and convincingly done, if the spectators are to go away satisfied. A different way—and Shakespeare's way—is to keep within the lines of preconceived impressions, and not to suppress or distort anything there may be in the way of recorded evidence, but to modify or intensify those impressions by giving the character a distinct personality of his own, neither whitewashing nor blackening him, but presenting him in something approximating, as far as possible, to his natural colours. To do this successfully is to produce an ultimate reaction of 'Why, yes—of course' in the spectator's mind, rather than the 'Yes, but . . .' that is so often the response to the other method when the immediate glamour of its presentation is beginning to wear off.

[1] *Our Theatres in the Nineties* (Constable, 1932), II, p. 291.

We have not, for the Chamberlain's Men, the wealth of documentation that is available for Henslowe's management, Very possibly their records and account-books were destroyed in 1613 in the famous fire at the Globe. Accordingly, we have no means of knowing whether the new company included *Henry VI* in its repertory, but in the circumstances it seems more than likely that it did. That play had closed with a couplet, and a flourish of sound, that had a ring of finality, as if the story were ended and left no occasion to expect anything more. It would be difficult indeed to suggest a continuance, or the need for one, after

> Sound, drums and trumpets, farewell sour annoy,
> For here, I hope, begins our lasting joy.

The opinion of A. W. Pollard was that Richard of Gloucester's self-revealing passages in this scene and before it were afterthoughts, written to pave the way for *Richard III*, and without necessarily accepting his contention that *Henry VI* itself is not by Shakespeare, we may suppose that the play as we have it represents the version performed by the Chamberlain's Men in 1594 and later. The first quarto of the *True Tragedie of Richard Duke of York* was not printed until 1595, but contains these extra bridge-passages, implying that they had been written into the play before the 1592 season at the Rose came to its abrupt end. As points on a graph guide one to the plotting of a curve, so we may trace, from these pieces of evidence, the possible development of the *Henry VI* cycle of plays.

First, suitably heralded, comes the original piece by the new author, with its combination of word-music and sensational scenes of violent and noisy action. It is a success from the first, and the author and management are encouraged to give the audience something more in the same vein. The Second and Third Parts follow in rapid succession, and the First Part is 'newly augmented' (to use a phrase beloved by the publishers of the Quartos) by the insertion of the Suffolk-and-Margaret scenes at the end. The parts are played as a trilogy, and once again it is clear that the story is worth carrying on. There is not much more to be done with Edward IV once he is anointed, crowned and set firmly in his throne with a son born to carry on his line, but a new character has come into prominence, and there are great chances for a play about the rise of the misshapen and unscrupulous Richard of Gloucester, particularly for Alleyn, who had just had a second part of *Tamburlaine the Great* written for him and must have been enjoying himself immensely. Once more, bridge passages are written in, to build up the character and give promise of tremendous things to come, and then everything is cut short by that unfortunate riot, the closing of the theatres, and the partial disintegration of the company. If *Richard III* had been written by that time, and had got so far as rehearsal, even if it had not received a performance, it would have been eagerly regarded as a money-maker by the renegades, botched up for performance by Pembroke's Men and ultimately published as a bad quarto like the others, but it was not. On the other hand, it must have been developing rapidly in its author's brain, and when Shakespeare went to the Chamberlain's Men, it was with a new play practically ready to be written.

All the same, it would have to be a play with a difference. For one point, the star part must be no longer conceived as an Alleyn part, but as a Burbage part, which was not at all the same thing. For another, the surge and thunder which had excited the relatively unsophisticated playgoers of Bankside was not sufficient for the citizens who had their shops and dwellings in the northern part of London and went to one or other of James Burbage's two theatres in Finsbury Fields. They were business men who appreciated reason as well as emotion, and who liked to be interested, not merely excited or disturbed. The new play is constructed on different lines from its preceding Histories, being designed to get its effect not solely by playing on the feelings, or by long passages of exposition, but by presenting evidence already familiar, in part at least, to the average reasonably-literate Londoner.

The section called 'The tragical doings of King Richard III' in Edward Hall's famous *Chronicle* is ascribed in the text to Sir Thomas More, and More was of an age, and in a position, to get much of his information from people who had been

Figure 2.—Typical London citizens, from Hogenberg's picture-map
of London, 1572.

(By courtesy of the Governors of the Museum of London.)

contemporaries, and sometimes eye-witnesses, of many of
the events described. Historical works were not only study-
material for the specialist but were popular reading-matter,
and Shakespeare's generation had grown up when Hall's
book was well established and Raphael Holinshed was just
bringing out his more comprehensive work, treating of
English history in general where Hall had concentrated
on the cause, progress and consequences of the Wars of the
Roses. To go back to our former simile, the account of this
reign provides graph-points numerous enough, and close
enough, for the rise and fall of Richard to be traced in a
reasonably firm and convincing curve, and to leave the
impression that the play is largely a presentation of
recorded fact. Indeed, the Elizabethans were better-read
in the Elizabethan chroniclers than a modern audience
can be expected to be, and we are apt, now and then, to
accord Shakespeare credit, or blame, for matters of presen-
tationthat were not the fruits of his own mind, but were
imposed on him, and on his audiences, by the sources that
were familiar to them all.

His treatment of his material, in this opening play for the great dramatic partnership, is worth considering in detail. With the very first sentences we can trace a difference in the character of its treatment, and the character and capacities of the actor for whom the title-part was written. It is quiet, almost conversational, opening with a soliloquy that tells the audience just where matters in England have got to, and at what point in the well-known history the play is about to begin. Burbage's vocal gifts were different from Alleyn's. The speeches in *Henry VI* in which Richard unburdens himself and declares his aspirations are typical Alleyn speeches, very much like those Marlowe wrote for him in *Tamburlaine* or the less familiar *Massacre at Paris*, where Alleyn must have stirred the audience with his delivery of the great monologue of Guise. Burbage obviously could not do that, and would be well advised not to try. He had seen and heard Alleyn often enough to know what each of them could or could not do, and there was no point in trying to be an imitation Alleyn, aiming at vocal effects that the older man could do better. He knew it, and Shakespeare knew it, and the new part was cut, accordingly, to the actor's measure.

It is a part that gives opportunities for subtle changes of character and of vocal modulation, and in both of these Burbage was proficient, as can be seen from the parts that are known to have been played by him. With this one, the beginning is the very antithesis of the sudden, arresting trumpet-notes of *Henry VI*. The long, slightly nasal opening vowel, the repetition of the w-sound, and the gentle relish of the succeeding consonants are followed by another long vowel and two sibilants with short vowels after them, and a concluding word that can roll off the tongue with quiet contentment,

> Now is the winter of our discontent
> Made glorious summer by this sun of York.

The lines, and those that follow them, are the very essence of tranquillity and contemplation, conveying a sense of hard work well done and well justified, and of a land blissfully at peace again under the summer sun.

Then the choice of one word—once again a word that can be drawn out with quiet relish—gives the auditor a slight touch of surprise. There is something detached, and not entirely sympathetic, in that remark about the *lascivious* pleasing of a lute. Next moment all contentment is gone, a cloud has passed over the sun and we awake with a shudder under the bitter wind of reality. '*But* I'—the heavy, explosive consonant and the drawn-out vowel jar and snarl like a bad gear-change, and are followed by phrase after phrase of savage alternative for the word that will not come. Twice in succession Richard evades it by saying what he is not, rather than what he is, then comes a cynical euphemism, 'rudely stamped', and another spirit of scorn for the majesty that he lacks, then two attempts at self-description, with a note of savage complaint at 'dissembling nature' that has cheated him, and at last there is nothing for it but the harsh, uncompromising word that he has been instinctively avoiding, and that conveys it all without further ado. That word 'deformed' would have been expressive at any stage of the speech, but is infinitely more so by the way it has been led up to. Now it is out, and the next few lines run more smoothly as an elaboration of it. Richard has revealed himself, and can take his hearers quickly and easily into his confidence. The 'glorious summer' of a few lines ago is mockingly recalled as a 'weak piping time'—once again one can hear the very vowels sneering—and it is much easier, this second time, to say the word 'deformity' with a grim acknowledgement of his obsession with it. Next moment there is another change. He has revealed himself, or at least as much of himself as he intends to, and having explained sufficiently what he is, he goes on to say with appalling candour what he is doing about it, and what he going to do. There are no poetic images now; the words are clear, expressive and come out with a certain businesslike efficiency, all the more alarming because of their lack of emotion. We have hardly been told of Richard's arrangements to discredit his brother Clarence when we see Clarence himself, with an armed guard about him, and realise that these arrangements are beginning to work, and that the mind behind them is something to be reckoned with.

'Dive, thoughts, down to my soul!'—one can almost hear the black thought go down like a plummet—'Here Clarence comes' and without a pause the key changes and the voice goes mildly on, with no more thundering consonants, but a tone of kindly, rather querulous enquiry. He is now very much the youngest of the brood, the little crippled brother to whom Clarence talks in an easy, patronising manner, being perplexed and quizzical about his position, where Richard seems to be anxious and disturbed. To hear the two of them talk, one would think that Clarence was by far the more dynamic and efficient. Richard is not egging him on to do anything, so his repeated 'we are not safe' need not have an edge to it, being no more than an expression— apparently—of personal apprehension. It is the more self-satisfied Clarence, the successful turncoat and opportunist, who begins to talk indiscreetly about the queen's family and to bring in the name of Jane Shore, mistress of the king and subsequently, if not simultaneously, of Lord Hastings, as if he were putting these ideas into his young brother's head, and not the reverse.

The reflective tone of Richard's next lines, and the rhyming couplet they contain, suggest an idea sinking in and accepted, and with a little start of intelligence he brings out a suggestion of his own as if it were not what Clarence had been practically explaining to him for the last few minutes. His sentiments, and his way of expressing them, are consistent, natural and not entirely unfamiliar, and are all the more plausible for that, since he is now giving a good imitation of the saintly Henry VI of the preceding play. After all, Clarence was not present when this man threw down the severed head of Somerset on the floor of the parliament-house, and Clarence's interests have always been centred on himself rather than of those about him. From the viewpoint of Brakenbury, in charge of the escort, the prisoner's conversation is likely to put unsuitable ideas into the head of the innocent Richard, and he very properly tries to put a stop to it. Richard affects to be deeply shocked—the word 'naught' in Shakespearean English meant not only 'nothing', but carried a suggestion of shocking or improper behaviour, surviving mildly to-day in the words 'naughty' and 'naughtiness'—and his 'Naught to do with Mistress Shore' comes out with the outraged propriety of a George Robey. In the earliest Quarto text, the joke ends here, with the couplet

> He that doth naught with her, excepting one,
> Were best to do it secretly, alone

and all its implications. By the time the Folio edition was printed, another line and a half had crept into the text, and taken matters a step further, Brakenbury being led into the indiscretion of asking 'What one, my lord?' and getting the indignant reply, 'Her husband, knave!—wouldst thou betray me?' as if it were Brakenbury who had been the first to hint at the king's relationship with the lady, and not the other way round. It is an ingenious elaboration of the position, and may well have sprung quite naturally from Burbage's playing of the scene.

Clarence is hastily marched off to the Tower, with an exchange of formal farewells and a promise of good intentions, and as soon as he is out of earshot the ring of the verse changes, and becomes at once sinister and contemptuous, with its

> Go, tread the path that thou shalt ne'er return,
> Simple, plain Clarence! I do love thee so
> That I will shortly send thy soul to Heaven
> —If Heaven will take the present at our hands.

That last line, cynically qualifying what has gone before, is a piece of characteristic Richard. Again and again he will be found relentlessly deflating his own remarks as readily as other people's, even in the tent at Bosworth on his last night alive.

Hastings, when he appears, is allowed to make the running from his very first cheerful greeting. Every time he speaks it is he who is making firm statements and expressing his opinions, and Richard who receives them all with grave acquiescence in what one may call his Henry VI manner, full of concern for the sick king's health and unavoidable regret that his way of life should have brought him to his present pass. Quite simply and unobtrusively the spectators have been shown the dangerous condition of both Richard's elder brothers, and as soon as Hastings is off the stage it is bluntly and cheerfully made clear to them that the really important thing is to make sure that the right one dies first. The lines are brisk, businesslike and grimly humorous when they refer to his intended wooing of Anne, making it bluntly clear that there is no nonsense about being in love with her. It is all for 'another secret close intent', she and her sister, Clarence's wife, having inherited the vast wealth of their father Warwick the King-maker. There is no Punch-and-Judy gloating here; the little speech is cast in simple matter-of-fact terms as if its appalling sentiments were purely commonplace and the course it outlines were the most natural thing in the world for any sensible man. Instead of impressive booming in the manner of Alleyn delivering a fine piece of Marlowe, the actor is being conversational and terrifyingly reasonable, as if taking for granted that everyone in the audience will agree with him. Reasonable, too, is the way in which he pulls himself up short and stops planning too far ahead. First things must come first, all this cannot happen until his two brothers are dead, and dead in the right order, so he goes bustling off to see about it, leaving the audience to recover from the speed of his personality and realise the implications of what they have seen and heard.

They are given ample opportunity to do so. As in music, this brisk, clear opening is followed by a slow movement, the funeral of the murdered Henry VI, attended by his widowed daughter-in-law Anne. The dragging syllables of her first line,

Set down, set down your honourable load,

convey something of the weariness and the weight, and the need for frequent pauses on the journey, when the bearers can be changed, and the slow course of the procession varied by an almost lyrical interlude of lamentation. Listening to it, we know who it is in the coffin, who the mourner is, and how her husband died, and we do not need to be told who killed them. Her solemn, detailed curse upon the murderer inclines us to prepare for its eventual fulfilment, and culminates in a supplementary curse on the woman whom he shall marry—and we have only just heard Richard explain to us who that will be. Then the load is taken up again, we are told where it is going, and why, and to all intents and purposes the little interlude is over.

Both visually and aurally, the next moment comes as a sudden shock. The ringing word 'Stay!', and the sudden appearance of Richard, break the tranquil flow of sound, with its drawn-out alliteration in 'And still, as you are weary of the weight' that accompanies the movement of the funeral procession getting under way again. The shock is an interruption, almost an outrage, and Lady Anne's exclamation

> What black magician conjures up this fiend
> To stop devoted charitable deeds?

comes out as a perfectly natural comment in the circumstances. A word like 'fiend' loses all its effect and meaning if cried out passionately at the end of a line, especially if it is followed by a word like 'to'. The 'ee' sound of the long vowel dulls the ear to the consonants that follow it, and the line carries *more* effect, not less, if spoken in a low tone of horror, and not hurried or shouted in an attempt to rival the tone of Richard's command. Anne is afraid, and for the next few moments, at any rate, the audience may be so too.

For this is a different Richard. We have seen him play the innocent, we have seen him wry-mouthed and sardonic, taking us into his unwanted confidence, but now he is growing in stature, dominating and menacing. There is no question of reverence for the dead; for him the body is an object-lesson and a warning for anyone who dares to oppose him.

> Villains, set down the corse, or by St. Paul
> I'll *make* a corse of him that disobeys.

This practice of repeating an important word in another context, or even merely echoing the sound of it, brings it home more emphatically to the hearers, and is employed by Shakespeare throughout his professional life, from the reiteration of the word 'king' in the first 10 or a dozen lines of his first known play, *I Henry VI.* Obviously Burbage made a good effect with this particular version of it, and Shakespeare gave him a chance to repeat it later, in a greater play, when Hamlet shakes off his companions, who are offering 'let or hindrance' to his attempt to follow the Ghost, with the words

By Heaven, I'll *make* a ghost of him that lets me!

One of the attendants has ventured to oppose him with levelled halberd, but quails before the calculated menace of the next three lines, especially when spoken low, as Baliol Holloway spoke them in 1924–25, standing motionless and supremely confident, with blazing eyes, and a suggestion of power that, if unleashed, could practically annihilate. It was not surprising that the halberd wavered in the man's hands, and went back slowly and obediently to the position of attention.[1] As a piece of stagecraft, the little episode contrives an opportunity for the guards and attendants to fall back a pace or two, leaving the field clear for the scene of direct conflict between Richard and Anne, while the movement is accelerated by her cry that the dead man's wounds are bleeding, as a victim's wounds were traditionally supposed to do in the presence of his murderer. The men would shrink back still further, not daring to approach, and mourner, murderer and victim would have the stage practically to themselves. Lady Anne continues her denunciation, but in a different tone. Before, her curse came as a solemn prayer for the punishment of a sinner; now it is an adjuration, practically a command, to heaven and earth to strike him dead at her feet.

The scene that follows is an extraordinarily effective blend of emotion and construction. Line answers line, couplet is balanced by couplet, and yet the effect is one not of artificiality, but of naturalness, for each answer seems to be the right one, the only one really possible. Even before Anne's last curse, we have had Richard's courteous protest 'Sweet saint, for charity be not so curst' receiving its answer,

[1]Almost exactly 50 years after that production, I mentioned this point to Esmond Knight, who had been playing Dorset in it, and found my impression vehemently corroborated. In addition to Dorset, he had been the halberdier in question, and swore he was 'scared stiff'.

'Foul devil, for God's sake hence, and trouble us not', and after her necessary pause for breath at the end of her tirade, he takes up his cue with all his former courtesy, beginning a duet that is almost operatic in its intensity and holds the interest of the audience not only by the tension of the drama but by the virtuosity of its form. It is the essence of so many contests, the necessity to follow suit at cards, to return a service at tennis with all speed, yet to keep within the court, to parry an attack and riposte from it with speed and grace— for in the fencing-school, as on the parade-ground, the prescribed way of carrying out a movement is the one calculated to achieve its end without waste of time or energy. Once, right at the beginning, Richard slips in an extra line, yielding momentarily to the temptation to deflate a senti- ment by a piece of cynicism at his own expense, when she answers his first couplet

> Lady, you know no rules of charity
> Which renders good for bad, blessings for curses,

with

> Villain, thou know'st no law of God nor man;
> No beast so fierce but knows some touch of pity

and he cannot resist capping her line with the argument

> But I know none, and therefore am no beast.

But this smart answering is an unsafe thing to do in the circumstances and throughout the scene he never does it again. His note consistently is, and must be, that of a repen- tant fiend pleading for redemption through the love of an angel. Shakespeare and Burbage were both familiar with Marlowe, and with Alleyn playing in Marlowe, with Faustus passionately trying to pray while the clock moves on towards the hour of his damnation, or Mephistophilis 'tormented with ten thousand hells' at the thought of the joys of Heaven that he knows are lost to him for ever. The scene is written in a way that gives the actor a chance to wring every possible drop of passion out of it. If Richard's tongue is in his cheek, he must not let it be seen there, or we shall think the less of Anne's intelligence that she does not see it too. It is in a pleading spirit that he now tries to play down his actions, notably excusing himself from blame for the death of her husband, on the grounds (to be remembered by those who had seen the preceding play) that though he admittedly stabbed him, it was Edward of York who had killed him already with his first blow.

The irregularity of the line about his next murder shows what a dramatic silence comes after her straightforward challenge 'Didst thou not kill this king?' Even so, he can bring himself to no more than an acquiescence, not a direct admission. His next few remarks, about the dead king's fitness for Heaven, are usually spoken with a sneer of contempt for Heaven and Henry alike, but it may be questioned whether this is not a mistake. To be wittily scornful here would be a tactical error on Richard's part, and undo much of what he has already achieved. Spoken 'straight', and in dead seriousness, the lines are at once an expression of very proper sentiment and, for a change, of agreement with Lady Anne instead of excuse or contradiction. For a moment, it seems, the two are united in one feeling of reverence for a good man, and Richard has got far enough to broach his next suggestion, and to meet her renewed flash of anger with the turned cheek and tears of penitence, leading up to them by a direct compliment to herself. Her accusation has ended with a sharp click of consonants

> Thou wast the cause and most accurst effect,

and in reply come two long, impressive vowels carrying words that she has not expected and cannot hear unmoved, especially as they are repeated to begin the next line as well—'Your beauty'. Spoken with great earnestness, the two words have a beauty of their own, and it is at this point that she really begins to waver in her resolution, leading up to the climax when she sees him on his knees before her and, with his own sword in her hand, she finds she cannot kill him. Her resolve has failed her, she is helpless and at a loss for comfort and reassurance, and that is what he gives her. There is a caressing tone about the words with which he slips his ring upon her finger, and begs to be allowed to take over the responsibilities of the funeral and wait upon her when he has

solemnly interred
At Chertsey monastery this noble king

(we have almost forgotten, at the moment, that it was he
who murdered him) and Anne takes her leave almost happy
in the thought of having reformed her demon lover. Burbage
has been given the chance to win over the lady *and the
audience* by the convincing way in which he expresses
himself, even as in a later play, at the end of Othello's great
speech before the Senate, the first thing anyone says after
it is the Duke's admission, 'I think this tale would win my
daughter, too'. That is how we ourselves must feel, till
Lady Anne is out of earshot and Richard is free to break
the spell.

He does it in two stages. First, when the bearers of the
body ask if they are to go on to Chertsey as arranged, they
are met with a brusque, blunt 'No', and told to take it to
Whitefriars and wait for him. Then, when at last he is alone,
he shows his real feelings in delighted mockery. First comes
the old 'woman wooed and won' antithesis, as we have had
it with Suffolk and Margaret in one play, and Demetrius and
Lavinia in another, with enough alliteration of vowels and
consonants to roll in relish from the tongue; next, with a
run of monosyllables, the pace quickens up for a moment
and relapses into a speech of reflection that balances the one
with which he opened the play, dealing in a very different
mood with the same subject—himself. We have already met
that word 'self' in the early stages of his passage-at-arms
with Lady Anne, when it was bandied about from one to
the other like a tennis-ball, and six times used to end a line,
and we shall meet it again, with similar echoing repetition
and more terrible significance, in the last act, when Richard
at midnight contemplates his approaching end. But here,
instead of bitter self-criticism and detestation, he finds he
has 'crept in favour with himself' and is cheerfully relishing
his grotesque appearance. There is no more thought of
'solemnly interring a noble king', or 'having best cause to
be a mourner'; he goes off to 'turn yon fellow in his grave'
and get on with his wooing. The more seriously and sincerely
he has played his love scene, the greater the effect of this

shocking piece of self-revelation, and we can understand a rude story, current in Shakespeare's lifetime and preserved for us in the diary of John Manningham for 1602, telling how a woman in the audience was so deeply impressed by Burbage's performance as Richard that before she left the theatre she made an amorous assignation with him for that evening. (Shakespeare overheard, got there first and took full advantage of it, announcing to the latecomer that 'William the Conqueror was before Richard III'.)

In the next scene he is back in his Henry VI mood, the injured innocent querulously complaining that he is being maligned. His sister-in-law and her brothers are in the ascendant and speak to him without serious apprehension, rather as if he were a troublesome child making spiteful remarks to his elders and having to be told that if this goes on they will have to speak to the king about it. Nonetheless, he continues to be irritatingly self-righteous among them all. There is nothing incisive or searing about the words he uses even under the lash of Queen Margaret's tongue. He is still 'too childish-foolish for this world', and remains consistently so, stirred to nothing stronger than mild protest or faintly priggish rebuke, and as a result, he alone is unaffected by the malevolence of her curses. The repeated aspirates in 'Have done thy charm, thou hateful withered hag', are no hammer-strokes, but more like suddering distaste, and the interjection by which he turns Margaret's curse upon herself seems a shocked, involuntary exclamation rather than the ingenious home-thrust that it is. Consistent throughout, he is able to utter unctuous excuses for her on her departure. Rivers, normally his opponent and his butt, is even moved to comment on his 'Christian-like conclusion' in praying for those who have wronged him, and it is only after dutifully replying 'So do I ever' that Richard at last relaxes enough to mutter a line and a half of secret self-appreciation, with his favourite 'myself' rounding off the remark.

In a moment he is alone, turning to the audience and inviting them to share his enjoyment and relish his technique, and with the entry of the murderers he is all simplicity again, but simplicity of a different kind. It is the cheerful man-to-man friendliness of a discerning employer with no nonsense

about him. There are aspirates again, but they no longer
come out sighing, there is a breezy, back-slapping tone about
'How now, my hardy, stout-resolved mates?' and the final
encouraging, 'I like you, lads; about your business straight'
that skates lightly over the fact that the 'business' is to be
the murder of his imprisoned brother.

That brother, in turn, is given his chance before he dies.
His speech to Brakenbury about his dream is a blend of
emotion and poetic imagery, in which an actor with a good
voice and keen intelligence can display them to the best
advantage. With Brakenbury he is emotional; with the
murderers, on the contrary, he is authoritative, after his
first moments of incredulity, and comes near to bearing
them down by the sheer force of his Plantagenet personality.
First he questions their authority in a stern and judicial
manner, as if he were checking them for a grave irregularity;
then, when told that 'he that hath commanded is the king'
he flashes back with Shakespeare's characteristic repetition
of the important word

> Erroneous vassals! the great *King* of kings
> Hath in the tables of his law commanded
> That thou—shalt—do—no—murder!

and at the end he is still not so much pleading against their
purpose as gravely advising them against it for their own
good. Indeed, he has just prevailed with the second murderer
when the first one kills him in something very like impulsive
panic. It is a scene of extraordinary dramatic tension, and
once again that tension is achieved by the author's appreciation of the sound of words as well as the sentiments behind
them.

Richard, when next we see him, is consistently in his
Henry VI impersonation at his brother's court, shocked and
grieved to be the bringer of bad news. King Edward's lines,
in the earlier part of this scene, have been easy to speak with
a sort of caressing relish. They are the words of a man weak
to the point of exhaustion, but still just able to express
his happiness at achieving an act of peace and reconciliation
before the end. The Folio text is surely right, however, in
giving to him, and not to Rivers, the sudden cry of incredulity

at the news of his brother's death. When Richard, in a tone of injured rebuke, says, 'Who knows not that the gentle duke is dead?' the reply, 'Who knows not he is dead! Who knows he *is*?' rings out with the sudden, hooting force of a man in the extremity of surprise and pain, while throughout the speech of reminiscence, when he has got control of himself again, the ever-recurring 'who—who—' becomes the sad moaning of a great man past his strength, who has neither the power nor, any more, the wish, to resist the approach of death. Shakespeare has not kept his verbal magic for Burbage alone; a good many of Richard's dupes and victims are allowed to display a little of it as they meet their end.

The mourning of the queen, the old duchess of York and the children of Clarence over Edward's death takes on again an operatic quality, voice answering voice antiphonally until the losses are all balanced and summed up by the aged duchess, and Dorset brings all to an end with the well-intentioned, priggish moralising of the young. Richard is still outwardly pious, but allows himself a sardonic little comment—very easy to murmur—on his mother's blessing, and an intimation, at the very end of the scene, that he and Buckingham have a certain mutual understanding that the others do not share. All the same, he does not put himself forward. As with Clarence at the very beginning, he is still the ignorant innocent, looking trustfully to the leading spirit. 'I, as a child, will go by thy direction', he says, and the very vowel-sounds have a smile in them. There is no need here to turn round and wink at the audience. They have seen the method in operation before, and are ready enough to wait for its results.

But Buckingham himself is not to keep his illusion long. In his next scene he meets with a new Richard, addressing his royal nephew with the respectful assurance of the grown-up person who always knows best, and showing his own contemporaries the balanced gravity of an Elder Statesman—which after all is not so very different. He is still playing second fiddle to Buckingham; it is Buckingham who gives orders to Catesby, and Richard does no more than endorse them. His valedictory, 'Shall we hear from you, Catesby, ere we sleep?' has the old caressing quality, and makes it all the more shocking to hear the change as soon as Catesby has gone. When Buckingham begins to deliberate what they had better do should Hastings be unwilling to join them, he gets an unexpected answer, quite brutal in its simplicity, 'Chop off his head, man, somewhat we will do'. There is no need for a change of vocal or facial expression; the words thesmelves carry the very stroke of the axe, and almost as alarming is the way the speaker dismisses the subject and turns at once to give instructions about something else. That has been quite enough; next moment the voice has once more a smile in it, and carries an invitation to discussions after an early supper. All the same, Buckingham has been warned.

We see and hear Richard in his Henry VI impersonation still, but with a difference. His words have a common-sense ring in them, as if the saintly Plantagenet were developing into the urbane but businesslike chairman of a company meeting. In the council-chamber he is gracious and pleasant to everyone, and with a complimentary remark about the bishop of Ely's strawberries he manages to delay the start of the meeting so that he can have a quick, private word with Buckingham, telling him that Hastings will not join their conspiracy against the new king. It is Buckingham who takes the initiative, and beckons him away to make arrangements accordingly, and it is by sound, not speech, that we learn in a few minutes what those arrangements are.

The business of the council, Richard's pleasant demeanour and the episode of the strawberries are described in the part of Hall's *Chronicle* that is acknowledged to have been written by Sir Thomas More. He, in his turn, got his information from Cardinal Morton, who had been bishop of Ely at the time and the actual owner of the strawberry-beds in question. The bishop was out of the room, sending for the strawberries, when Richard and Buckingham absented themselves, and Hall's account says that Richard was away for more than an hour, but on his return the narrative becomes a straightforward account of what Morton saw and—still more dramatically—what he heard. The lords had noticed, as they do in the play, Richard's extreme friendliness and good temper, but he came back

> all changed, with a wonderful sour angry countenance,
> knitting the brows, frowning and fretting and gnawing
> on his lips, and so set him down in his place. All the
> lords were dismayed, and sore marvelled   of this
> manner and sudden change, and what thing should
> him aid.

That sudden change is well marked in the lines and theatrically effective on the stage, with its abrupt opening question,
the baring of the Protector's undeveloped forearm, the
accusation of the queen and Jane Shore, and finally of
Hastings himself, culminating in the terrible word 'traitor'
with all its implications of the strangling rope, the still-
living body taken down and 'drawn' like a fowl, and the
limbs set up over the gates of London to the mercy of the
weather and the carrion-birds.

The mind cannot usually concentrate on visual and aural
impressions at the same time. Sounds, when they reach the
consciousness, can linger in the memory longer and more
clearly than recollections of things actually seen, and More's
account of what follows is an account of sounds, rather than
sights, over the next few moments.

> And therewith (as in a great anger) he clapped his
> fist on the board a great rap, at which token given,
> one cried treason without the chamber, and therewith
> a door clapped, and in came rushing men in harness as
> many as the chamber could hold.

Morton, More and Shakespeare in his turn must have been
stirred by the memory or imagination of that sequence of
sound—the 'great rap' of a hand upon the council-board, the
answering cry from outside, the clatter of a door dashed
back against the wall, and the sudden inrush of armed men.
Indeed, it looks as if Shakespeare had been so deeply
impressed by it that he had employed it already in *Henry VI*,
once in the First Part when the sound of Talbot's horn brings
his troops to storm the gates of the countess of Auvergne,
and more recently in the Third Part, where the hidden
soldiers appear in the parliament-house at the stamp of
Warwick's foot. Neither of these episodes is recorded by

the chroniclers; the dramatist put them in, presumably, to make use of a good dramatic effect, and it was worth using again in its proper context. When the sound stops, and the councillors look round and see the menacing figures about them (and possibly Stanley with a slight head-wound, as Hall records and Hastings in his final speech appears to hint at), Richard's words take on another tone. They are still ruthless, but not tempest-tossed by passion, they are no longer menacing, except perhaps in the exit line; instead of being orders brilliantly conceived in an emergency, they are instructions given by someone in the unquestionable certainty that they will be carried out. The speaker's point is not that the deed shall be done, but that it shall be done efficiently, and at once, and reported to him afterwards. The content of the speech is given by Hall, but the marshalling of the words is Shakespeare's, and he and the player between them gain their effect in no more than four lines:

> Off with his head!—now by St. Paul I swear
> I will not dine until I see the same.
> Lovel and Ratcliff, look that it be done,
> The rest, that love me, rise and follow me.

He leads them out, and there is every justification for a pause of silence here, to allow Hastings—and the audience— to recover from the shock, before the slow, sad cadences of his 'Woe, woe for England, not a whit for me' and the reflections that follow it. Not only does the situation require, and the lines provide, a slowing-down of the whole pace of the scene; Richard and Buckingham, in the tiring-house, need as much as time as possible to put on what the Folio stage-direction calls 'rotten armour, marvellous ill-favoured', and the history itself describes as 'some old ill-favoured briganders' that were among the odds and ends in the Tower. A 'brigander'—better known as a brigandine—was a close-fitting jacket lined with small overlapping plates of iron which were fastened by rivets to their textile covering. If the latter rotted, with age or damp, the rivet-heads would tear through it here and there, the plates would slip, and the whole garment look very shabby indeed. Its virtue, both for military and for theatrical purposes, was that it was all of a piece, and could be put on in less time than would be taken by the strapping and buckling of a plate cuirass.

These, then, are the garments that Richard and Buckingham put on, and in which they make their grotesque appearance. Their lines of grim comedy provide a sudden change from the terror and tragedy that have gone before, and Richard indulges his Henry VI impersonation to the full for the benefit of the Lord Mayor, who goes away fully persuaded, and ready to persuade any other enquirer, that they have acted reluctantly but efficiently, and saved themselves and their country in a dangerous situation.

As soon as he has gone, the tone changes to one of speed and efficiency, with its 'Go after, after, cousin Buckingham', and a quick yet detailed briefing on what he is to say at Guildhall, how far he is to go in blackening the dead king's character, where he is to go next and what he may expect to find there. Lovel and his companion are sent on their various errands, and Richard gives the audience a rapid intimation of his own next moves, before he hurries away to get out of his armour during the Scrivener's monologue that follows. This is necessarily slow and contemplative, for its arguments (all out of Hall again) must be allowed to sink in. Not only does it give time for the actor's quick change, but it illustrates yet more plainly the alarmingly efficient planning that has been at the back of Richard's words and actions. He knows what he is about, and his designs are successful when he is there to control them, though the next scene shows that they are not so when left to other people. Buckingham's explanation of his own Guildhall speech is full of detailed arguments, as if he had thought of them himself and not been carefully instructed by Richard, and he ends by giving instructions on his own account, ignoring the fact that Richard has arranged already for the attendance of 'reverend fathers and well learned bishops' and has told him so. His master says very little, but lets him go on, directing the whole business as if it were his own idea, and duly makes his 'positively last appearance' in the character of a humble, saintly prince, unversed in worldly affairs and very reluctantly accepting the burden of worldly honour, so that the act ends with his consenting, almost sadly and under protest, 'even when you please, for you will have it so', to be crowned King of England.

Chapter Five

BURBAGE ENTHRONED

WE NOW SEE HIS WIFE, his mother and his brother Edward's widow receiving the news of his advancement. Once again, as after the king's death, their lamentations have an antiphonal, operatic quality. The widowed queen is full of fear and apprehension for her children in the Tower and their half-brother, Dorset, still fortunately out of it, the duchess of York is almost broken with age and horror at this further enormity of her son, and Anne's lines combine passionate feeling with sheer wretchedness and despair. There is no protest, the thing is upon her, unavoidable and terrible, and there is nothing left but to bear it to the end. Still clear in memory is the voice of Angela Baddeley, in an otherwise unmemorable production, saying

> Anointed let me be with deadly venom
> And *die*, ere men can say God save the Queen!

and the revulsion she put into the last four words, conveying at the same time the certainty that there would be no escape. Sadly she accepts her fate as the consequence of her early curse upon the woman King Henry's murderer should marry, and her own credulity in becoming that woman herself, while in her closing lines she not only foretells her own death by Richard's design—which we have just heard of, by his own curt admission—but gives us our first intimation of those 'timorous dreams' that disturb him in the night-time and show that even his indomitable nerve is beginning to crack.

The scene has given time for Burbage to get into his robes and crown, and we see him in full state, being handed up into his throne by Buckingham. From the first moment there is a contrast between sight and sound. Richard has at last come to the 'golden time' he looked for, and his mind, after all, is filled with uncertainty. King Edward's two little sons, the rightful heirs, are yet living, in the Tower. He feels he is not safe, and will not be safe, until something still more is done, and yet cannot bring himself to admit, in so many words, what that something is. For a few moments we are back at that first speech of all, when he was so reluctant to call his deformity by its true name.

Alleyn, if the play had been written for the Admiral's Men, would have had had a speech here in which he could 'threaten the world in high astounding terms'. For Burbage, less trumpet-tongued, the occasion is one for deeper insight

Figure 3.—Figure of Tamerlane, from Knolles's *History of the Turks*. The dress, wig and features combine to suggest that it is in fact a portrait of Alleyn as the Tamburlaine of Marlowe's play.

and keener subtlety. The very injunction at the opening, 'Stand all apart', sets the note for the conversation that follows, and turns it, though every word is audible, into a matter of whispering and secrecy in the middle of all the splendour. Richard knows what he wants, but shrinks from putting it into words, and does all he can to induce Buckingham to say it first.

But Buckingham, hitherto so ready to act on Richard's ideas and give himself the credit for them, is not going to play the leader now. Richard's hints and short, jerky half-sentences have to lead on to one savage, sibilant admission, 'Shall I be plain? I wish the bastards *dead,*' and even then, this draws no more than a non-committal admission that 'Your Grace may do your pleasure'. There is one more attempt, a flattering pretence of consultation, in 'Say, have I thy consent that they shall die?', but Buckingham will not readily commit himself, and begs leave to withdraw for a moment and think about it. What he does not realise is that he has been the catspaw, not the leader, throughout the whole business, and that once he has begun to hesitate, Richard has no further use for him. Richard himself seems to gain resolution from the fact. Buckingham is written off as unserviceable, a page is summoned to get him a 'discontented gentleman' from somewhere else, and Catesby is given instructions to spread the rumour that the unhappy Anne is 'sick, and like to die'. Richard himself will arrange the rest. At once he begins to discuss his next marriage. As before, once the unpalatable item is swallowed, the rest of the dish may be tackled with confidence. He is 'so far in blood that sin will pluck on sin', and having admitted as much, will not waste any time on pity, for himself or for anyone else concerned.

There is no more hesitation; when Tyrell is brought to him he uses little beating about the bush, but says in a brief and businesslike manner what he wants done, and what the arrangements are for doing it. Once that is concluded, he turns his mind to the next problem, and gives Stanley a word of warning about his stepson, the earl of Richmond, who may have to be dealt with next if he becomes a serious danger to the throne. It is an unsuitable moment for

Buckingham to come back and intrude on this serious conference with the news that he has made up his mind about
something that the king has now settled quite efficiently
without him. Worse still, he goes on to pester him about an
early promise of the earldom of Hereford and the late king's
personal belongings. After ignoring his first few interruptions,
Richard turns suddenly on him and for a moment becomes
the menacing demon whose appearance had brought king
Henry's funeral to a halt. In faint protest, Buckingham tries
to insist upon an answer of some sort, but is cut short by one
ominous line, 'Thou troublest me; I am not in the vein'.
Before he can recover, the king has stormed away, with the
court after him, and Buckingham is left apprehensive and
alone. The king's face and the king's favour have been turned
from him for ever, and we shall never see Buckingham again
till he is led out to die.

Tyrell opens the next scene with a passage of emotional
narrative describing the murder of the two little princes. His
ready acceptance of the commission is forgotten in his
revulsion at the memory of the actual deed and the necessity of reporting it to the king. The passion of the speech
renders doubly horrible the silky, caressing line in which
Richard questions him—'Kind Tyrell, am I happy in thy
news?' The answer comes almost reluctantly and incredu-
lously

> If to have done the thing you gave in charge
> Beg your happiness, be happy then,
> For it is done.

There is no overt criticism in it, but it is the voice of a man
who feels that he himself will never know happiness again.

Richard is delighted. He presses for details, sees that
Tyrell is in no fit state to give them and defers the full
description till after supper. Once he is alone his tone is
cheerful, reflective and consistently businesslike. He is now
the capable statesman with no foolish illusions, enumerating
his various nephews and nieces and the steps he has taken,
or proposes to take, to deal with them, including the removal
of his own wife, so that he can marry the niece who otherwise might (and ultimately did) marry his cousin Richmond

and strengthen the latter's claim to the crown. Sudden news of Morton's departure and Buckingham's active rebellion is met with quick assessment, decision, and something more, the heartening exultation of a king ready to lead his people to victory. There is to be an end of scheming and planning; what next has to be done must be done quickly and surely, and the use of two rhymed couplets, so widely differing in sound and implication, rounds off the scene with a sense of urgency without confusion, the right words falling unerringly into the right places at the right moment. It is a time for speed, but not for panic, and for a moment Burbage's voice could take on the sound of a royal bugle calling England to arms.

> Then fiery expedition be my wing,
> Jove's Mercury, and herald for a king,

But that is not to serve as an exit-line. There is a couplet of brisk, cheering instruction to Ratcliff, who has brought the tidings.

> Go muster men; my counsel is my shield;
> We must be brief when traitors brave the field.

For a moment we are shown yet another Richard. That piece of short conversation, putting new heart into a subordinate with the approach of danger, illustrates the instinctive understanding of other men's feelings which is one of the features of good leadership. We have seen Tyrell shudder at king Richard only a few minutes back; now, in the very same scene, we are faced unexpectedly with a sight of qualities that could make men trust and like him.

This sudden lilt of energy and exhilaration prepares the way for his appearance at the head of his troops. Meanwhile there is another interlude of musical speech and answer, when two former queens and the aged duchess raise their voices in lamentation and reckoning. The scene is deliberately static, and is borne up by the verse-speaking alone, without the intrusion of movement to disturb the harmony. Once again, as in their mourning for Edward, the noble ladies of York match grief for grief and loss for loss, but this time they are joined by the relentless voice of

Lancaster in the person of the fallen Amazon who had been
Margaret of Anjou. Where their harmony is that of comparison, hers is that of contrast. She is not only the
Margaret of the Henry VI plays, whose fatal marriage had
brought about the downfall of Henry's house; she is not even
stirred to cursing-point by passionate hate, as in her earlier
entry in the present play; she is without passion and without
pity, for she has exhausted them all. It is worth remembering
that before writing this play, and after the scene of young
Edward's murder on the stricken field of Tewkesbury,
Shakespeare had created Tamora, another woman who had
pleaded vainly for her son, had seen him led away to be
butchered in cold blood, and when later appealed to, in
her turn, to show some pity, could reply implacably, 'I
know not what it means'. It is this contrast of feeling that
gives the scene life, where agreement would make only for
monotony. She has one or two brief imprecations upon
Richard, but for the most part she is exhausted with the
fulfilment of her revenge, and can take a courteous leave of
her once-successful rival, who appeals to her for a lesson in
the art of cursing. When, at the end of all, the queen cries

> My words are dull: O, quicken them with thine!

the answer echoes the last word, and carries in its long
vowels a note of almost kindly reassurance and encouragement,

> Thy woes will make them sharp, and pierce, like mine.

With that, she is gone from them, and a few lines later they,
and the audience, are suddenly recalled to the needs of the
moment by the sound of Richard's drum.

The interlude has given him time to put on his armour,
and with it to put on another personality, that of England's
king leading his troops into the field against a threatening
enemy. When his mother and sister-in-law stand in his path
and assail him with reproaches, he answers them not with
personal anger, but with authority, as one who has right on
his side, and has urgent work to do. As far as time allows
him, he will be patient, and he still treats his mother with
courtesy under provocation, but he insists that she must

speak briefly and to the point, if she is to be allowed an
interview at all. He turns one of her reproaches into a joke
by giving apparent agreement, as usual echoing the sound of
her line except for the widely-differing word where the
stress comes, the words 'in thy company' being balanced by
'forth of my company', but as she has nothing to do but
rail at him, he prepares, sharply, but not discourteously,
to end the interview and go on his way. Even now, on her
last appeal, he reluctantly agrees to listen to her, and finds
that all she has to give him is a curse. It is a great change
from the blessing he received so hypocritically, and he
receives it in silence, letting her make her exit on the final
rhyming couplet without any comment to sent her on her
way.

The scene that follows is apt to be criticised as a mere
repetition of Richard's wooing at the beginning of the
play, and is often cut down, or even omitted, on that
account. Examination of it in detail, however, suggests very
strongly that this is a mistaken view. Richard is doing the
same thing as before, or something very like it, but he is
dealing with a different woman, and goes about his task in
a very different way. Elizabeth of York is exhausted and
miserable; she has none of her mother-in-law's toughness
(the old lady had been known as 'proud Cis of Raby' in
her younger days) and she wants no more than to go away
and hide her sorrow in seclusion, but Richard has other
plans. There is a compliment in his opening line to her,
indicating that unlike her mother she is someone he wants
to talk to, on an important matter of business. There is
nothing here of the lost soul crying out of hell-fire for
redemption; this time he is a king and a statesman, qualified
to understand the national situation better than she can,
and consequently to advise her for her own good, and
England's. Where she is passionate, he is calm; where she
makes wild—and justified—accusations, he is infinitely
patient, and prepared to make allowances, letting her charges
pass not without answer but with explanation rather than
resentment. The voice he puts on now is the voice of grave
wisdom, and the insidious flattery with which he beguiles
her is his apparent conviction that she herself is an intelligent

woman, qualified in her turn to understand his point of
view when once it is explained to her. From the line-by-line
passage at the beginning, in which each of his advances is
parried and met with an indignant riposte, sometimes with
a jingling echo of his own words, he manoeuvres her
gradually into a position of serious, man-to-man discussion
in which he seems to be considering her grievances, explaining her own position and asking her, quite frankly, for her
advice. The place of quick statement and reply is taken by
a long, careful speech with an unexpectedly modern opening
that startles her into silence.

> Look, what is done cannot be now amended:
> Men shall deal unadvisedly sometimes
> Which after hours give leisure to repent.

He is admitting his usurpation of the kingdom, he is even
admitting the murder of her little sons, but, even more
incredibly, he is admitting that he has not, perhaps, acted
very wisely. He has made a bad mistake, and would be
glad of her help to set it right, so far as this can be done
at all. He could not have armed his hook with a better
bait.

It is still the technique of a Government department that
has made a wrong decision, has been forced to admit it,
and has no intention of righting the wrong. Her first
indignant repudiation is calmly disregarded; again and again
he presents her with sound, reasonable arguments, backing
them by oaths which she refuses to believe, until the
culmination comes with his detailed imprecation upon
himself if he should not now be acting in good faith. His
earnestness is all-compelling, and leads once more to a
warning of what might happen to them all if this marriage
is not accomplished for the sake of the country's peace.
Listening to the sound of his words, we can almost feel, as
he feels, her resolution wavering, and he quietly presses
home his advantage with grave reiteration and a note of
absolute, uncompromising certainty.

> It cannot be avoided but by this;
> It *will* not be avoided but by this;

He has transferred the responsibility to her shoulders, and he knows exactly when to stop. There is no more urging; he ends with a request for her sympathy and help. The old 'self' jingle appears again in her wavering replies, and is gravely and reassuringly answered. At last she goes, persuaded by his argument and prepared to further his designs, and we are all shocked back into realisation of the true state of things by Richard's single line of comment on the whole affair,

Relenting fool, and shallow, changing woman!

All the same, the episode has taken more out of him than he would care to admit. It has interrupted, and brought to a standstill, that swift, efficient action that was his original antidote to Ratcliff's news about Morton and Buckingham, and he has at once to get things moving again and make up for lost time. There is nothing now of his usual clear-sighted, driving efficiency, sweeping onward towards a definite goal and carrying his followers with him on the wind of his enthusiasm. He is flustered and uncertain, snapping out orders to his officers to go to this place or that, without telling them what to do there, and striking a messenger without waiting to hear his news—which turns out to be good news, for a change, and has to be rewarded with an equally impulsive gift. This is no longer the cold, menacing nobleman who could dominate a whole funeral procession by his concentrated malevolence; the very act of striking, and striking the wrong man for the wrong reason, shows that the man's grasp is slipping, and he is losing his absolute control of his own design. Again and again he calls for instant action, but it is no longer with the heartening enthusiasm of the leader who has sprung readily to arms at the approach of danger. His obsession with time, and with the need for haste, underlines the significance of the long scene that has gone before. By coming in when they did, and necessitating that amount of careful argument and persuasion, the mourning ladies have checked his impulse, cooled his initial energy and left him, in Margaret's own words, 'but the very prey to time'.

When at last he and his army move off to Salisbury, their joyous enthusiasm has given place to the anxiety of

men desperately in haste to recover the initial advantage
they have lost, and apprehensive that they may never do so.
Even the news of Buckingham's capture does little or nothing
to relieve it. Colley Cibber's famous interpolation 'Off with
his head—so much for Buckingham!' has an effective sound,
and many Richards have enjoyed declaiming it, but it is dead
against the situation Shakespeare has so ingeniously built
up. Richard is no longer master of himself and of events, and
capable of making immediate decisions. He is in a hurry and
cannot even detail any particular person to look after
Buckingham—and, as a final point, he is not given a ringing,
rhyming couplet to take him and his army off the stage.
The effect, gained not only by dramatic construction but
by the choice of words and the framing of sentences, is one
of haste, uncertainty and demoralisation.

After the tensions and emotions of this long scene, it is a
relief to enjoy a little straightforward exposition for a
change. Stanley's messages to the earl of Richmond, to be
delivered to him by the priest Urswick, inform the audience
of Stanley's own position and willingness to join the earl
were it not for his son's being held as a hostage. The very
fact that the speech is conversational makes it easier for its
contents to be understood, and shows that a scene may be
unemotional without necessarily being undramatic, while
in the little scene that follows, the last moments of Buckingham indicate what may be in store for Stanley and his son
should his true feelings be detected. Here, surely, rather
than between the two scenes (where the Folio puts it)
is the true pause and breathing-space between act and act,
ending with the sonorous, knell-like reminder that

Wróng hath but wróng, and bláme the due of bláme.

The placing of a brief pause here gives the action of the
play more shape. The audience can relax for a few moments
of thought, comment and refreshment. It was not as if they
had the time, wish or ability to leave their seats, break the
tension entirely and crowd into the bars—from which, in a
modern theatre, it takes so much time to get them back to
their places. For the most part, people ate or drank what
they had brought with them, like the gentleman many years

later who used bottle-ale to put out his burning breeches when the Globe caught fire in 1613. All that was really needed was a slackening of the intense concentration of the past few scenes, in readiness for a proper appreciation of what comes next.

What *does* come next is a complete change from what has gone before. The audience is confronted with new sights, new sounds and new sentiments from the very opening of the scene. The arresting introduction of 'drum and colours' ushers in a group of people who have not hitherto appeared, and their leader addresses them in cheerful tones with news of 'fair comfort and encouragement'. The tide has turned, the deliverer has come, in the form of Stanley's correspondent, that earl of Richmond of whom we have heard at intervals in the preceding acts. In the most natural way in the world, the speaker indicates where Richard is, where he himself is, and what chance there is of deciding the fate of England in one sharp, sudden battle. His officers prophesy that Richard's own friends will quite possibly change sides—which a good many of them actually did—and Richmond goes off with just such a ringing couplet as Richard had lacked when he was last seen moving off to battle.

Richard himself, when we see him again, has recovered his efficiency and is full of bustling energy and encouragement, cheering his officers with promises of success and at the same time seeing that everything possible is done to secure it. There is one significant change, however. In one line—only one, and that not spoken to any of those about him—he admits to the possibility of something else, and grimly avoids further consideration of it, going on at once to an enquiry about the size of the opposing forces. Still, for the first time we have seen him not absolutely confident of his own ability and consequent success.

On an Elizabethan stage, with little or no pictorial scenery, and before an Elizabethan audience, which had no individual programmes to consult as a matter of course, it was doubly and trebly important for the words to set the scene and identify the various characters and their states of mind. Here, in particular, where the leaders of the opposing armies have to appear turn and turn about in the same acting area, there must be no doubt of the identity and feelings of the armed men occupying the stage, and the author's word-music does much to differentiate them. Richard's utterances are jerky, broken and addressed now to one and now to another, leaving no doubt of the urgency of the position, and the underlying anxiety behind it. Richmond, when he appears, has a speech of long, flowing uninterrupted lines, combining strength with calm, and from their very first words calling up the image of a long, golden evening affording rest at the end of a tiring but not unfruitful day. Where the language of the usurper has been a torrent dashing down among rocks this is

> Such a tide as moving seems asleep,
> Too full for sound or foam,

and having something of the calm, inexorable certainty of the incoming sea. There is no sign or doubt or desperation, the smallness of the force is admitted from the first, but only to ensure that it is disposed to the best possible advantage, and in the absence of stage lighting-effects the words themselves have to suggest the passing of time and the sudden chill that comes at the end of such a day. The sun has set while Henry is speaking, and it is no longer warm enough for discussions in the open air.

This advance of time is immediately echoed in the opening of the next scene. Richard is restless and uneasy, full of injunctions about details that might be taken for granted, and making sudden remarks to Norfolk and Ratcliff as if he could not bring himself to let them leave him. The repeated enquiry for ink and paper suggests that he does not mean to go to sleep, but to sit up writing far into the night, and in any event Ratcliff is to call him at midnight and help him to make ready. He is uncertain about the morale and loyalty of his troops, and relieved to hear that Northumberland and Surrey have gone the rounds to put new heart into the men. Here, perhaps, we may even guess at a piece of stage positioning. Richard has asked for a bowl of wine, and Ratcliff has moved away to get it, so that Richard is able to admit to himself that he is not so quick and self-confident as usual. Next moment he realises that Ratcliff

I *Self-portrait of Richard Burbage, in Dulwich College Picture Gallery.*
(By permission of the Governors of Dulwich College
Picture Gallery)

II *A Franciscan at Prayer, by Francisco Zurbaran (1598–1662).*
(By courtesy of the Trustees, The National Gallery, London.)

III *Richard Tarlton, the famous Elizabethan clown, from whom Armin learnt his art. From an elaborate initial in the British Library, MS. Harl. 3885. (See p. 204). Reproduced by permission of the British Library Board.*

IV *King Henry VIII towards the end of his life. Contemporary copy of a portrait by Holbein.*

(*By gracious permission of H.M. The Queen.*)

is at his side again, handing him the cup, almost ready to
overhear his inmost thoughts, and with sudden revulsion
he orders him to put it down and go away. In his present
mood it is better, and safer, for him to be alone.

All this anxiety and apprehension serve to mark the
contrast of the following scene, where Henry of Richmond
is visited by his stepfather Stanley under cover of night.
The very first words are 'Fortune and victory', the whole
opening line is a message of good will, and the one after
it speaks at once of comfort and the dark, instinctively
suggesting the passage of time. Indeed, Stanley's next few
lines carry on the idea with their intimation of the approach
of morning. There is something curiously expressive in the
combination of long, quiet vowels and repeated k-sounds
after a half-line of stillness and anticipation. With the words

> The silent hours steal on
> And flaky darkness breaks within the east

one gets the sense that the impenetrability of night is no
longer holding together, the darkness is breaking up and we
must very soon be ready for the first light of dawn. How
much of this is deliberate word-selection we cannot tell. It
looks, and sounds, more as if the words had presented themselves to the writer's mind as suggested by the feeling, than
suggesting it. Be it instinctive inspiration or deliberate choice,
the lines convey the right image at the right moment, and
we must accept the fact and be thankful.

Now comes what is perhaps the best-known scene in the
play, when the ghosts of Richard's victims appear in the
order in which he killed them. The use of pictorial scenery
has handicapped the staging of this, from the 18th century
onwards, because the setting in Richard's tent makes it
difficult to arrange for the presence of his rival. Sometimes
it is stylised, with the two tent-openings put cheek-by-jowl,
like bathing-huts on a beach, sometimes the lines of
encouragement to Richmond are spoken into the wings,
very often they are completely cut. Recollections of the
unlocalised Elizabethan stage have been invoked to justify
the playing of the scene with both sleepers visible at once,
but it may be queried whether the original idea was not to

play it with neither, leaving the acting-area to the ghosts alone. The usual sight of Richard writhing, groaning and muttering on his bed, distracting one's attention from the ghosts but never actually addressing them, is apt to seem longer than it need be, because while the ghosts are different, Richard's reactions to all of them are the same. Macbeth's confrontation with the shadowy kings in a still greater play, where the ghosts are silent but Macbeth has a remark for each, shows what Shakespeare could do, when he wanted, with such an accumulation of phantoms, but there is no call for him to do so here. If we are not continually distracted by the sight and inarticulate sounds of the dreamer, we are free ourselves to concentrate upon the dream. For a few minutes we can *be* Richard, we can see what he sees, hear what he hears, and be relentlessly reminded of things that he would give almost anything to forget.

In this way, it seems perfectly logical and justifiable to introduce the ghosts of two people who have not been killed in this play at all, for Richard's career of murder and murderous conspiracy began with his stabbing of the captured prince on Tewkesbury field, and his hurried departure from thence 'to make a bloody supper in the Tower'. After those first two personal victims, we are shown in succession those whom he sent to death at the hands of others, by the malmsey-butt, the smothering pillows or the executioner's axe, and the pitiful figure of one whose death is attributed to him, whether by insidious poison or from simple wretchedness and despair. Small as these parts are, they show in their turn the contrast between the consonantal hammer-strokes of their address to Richard, with its reiterated 'Despair and die', and the smooth, flowing periods in which they give their blessing to his enemy.

Suddenly the tranquility of the scene is broken by a combination of sound and violent, convulsive movement as, in the words of the stage-direction, 'King Richard starts out of his dream'. Just such an entry, in not very different circumstances, is made by the guilty Mathias in the last scene of *The Bells,* the melodrama that first made Irving's name and ultimately, to all intents and purposes, killed him. Many of us have read, or have heard from our elders, how electrifying was the sudden appearance of the dreamer as he burst through the curtains of his bed with his cry of 'Take the rope from my neck!', some of us will remember the same moment in Martin-Harvey's revival of the play. Even so, it may be conjectured, may Shakespeare's audience have been startled into sudden alarm when Burbage first broke through the hangings and fell with a crash upon the stage.

His first line suggests that he may indeed have arrived headlong, and be scrambling up from his hands and knees. He has fallen out of bed in a nightmare, and his first confused impression is that he is on the battlefield, thrown from his horse and in imminent danger of death. After that first cry to his colleagues and his God, he comes gradually to himself, and with an almost equally sharp contrast the sound of the scene changes to the quiet of the dark.

There was no dark upon the day-lit stage of the Theatre or the Globe. In consequence, the audience could see quite plainly the faces and appearance of the ghosts, and hear all the more clearly what they had to say. So, in turn, when Richard says 'The lights burn blue' we are not distracted by seeing them do it and wondering how, or noticing—and subconsciously resenting—that they do nothing of the sort. Where there is no question of expecting such a stage-effect, the actor's allusion to it is quite enough. Burbage, alone upon the stage, would be clearly visible, and all the more clearly recognisable as a man surrounded, and terrified, by the empty darkness which he conjures up by the way in which he speaks of it.

With all respect to a distinguished Shakespearean scholar, one may yet question whether Lord Evans is fully justified in his assertions that in this scene 'Shakespeare seems to have no effective linguistic instrument at hand'[1] and that 'in one of the most crucial moments in the play the verse falters, and interest is maintained solely by the situation'. For one thing, the author has deliberately worked up the play to this situation, and it is the situation, not the verse, that must excite, and hold, the interest of the audience. And, for

[1] B. Ifor Evans, *The Language of Shakespeare's Plays* (Methuen, 1952).

another, Shakespeare had indeed a most effective linguistic instrument at hand, and its name was Burbage. His voice may not have been thundrous—there is every indication that it was not—but there can be no question that it was expressive, and never more so than here, where the struggles of fear are met again and again with the hard logic of inescapable, unpalatable fact. Whatever the setting, whatever the lighting, when the right kind of voice can say, out of the silence,

> Cold fearful drops stand on my trembling flesh

we can believe very readily that they do. The very necessity to avoid slurring the sibilants means that each word may have to come out individually, and let its meaning sink in without slackening the tension of the line.

And with the next line comes a word that has been the real centre of Richard's creed throughout the play. The scene of his wooing of Anne showed his obsession with the thought and the sound of 'self'; again and again, in later scenes, the word had come up again at appropriate moments, and always as if Richard's own self were something that he could take out and contemplate with approval in the manner of Peer Gynt. Now, however, there is an echo of an earlier use, in the closing scene of *Titus Andronicus,* with its recognition of the ominous fact that one can be proof against all enemies except, in the last instance, oneself, and that self-interest has the best and easiest opportunities for self-destruction. It is the vocal tone that can best convey the shifts and changes of mental attitude, the natural apprehension in 'Is there a murderer here?', the reassuring 'No', and then the hard, literal truth and the realisation that wherever he is, there will always be a murderer in the room. His admission 'I am a villain' is followed at once by a swift, self-justifying denial and the sharp, angry self-rebuke 'Fool, of thyself speak well' and, on the heels of that, the cold, uncompromising scorn of 'Fool, do not flatter'. The time for self-deception is past, the end is at hand and there is nothing left. 'There is no creature loves me', he cries, and no one to pity him at his death, and with the awful, uncompromising candour that has characterised his earlier enormities he admits that there is no reason why anybody should. More than once he has prided himself on being incapable of pity, and even in this, his last extremity, he cannot feel it now. For a moment or two, when Ratcliff comes to arm him, he admits to being distrubed, uncertain and afraid, and that is as far as he will go. Even with the words, he pulls himself together and arranges to go round the lines and listen for any signs of disaffection among his officers.

When next we see him, he has been doing so, and is now questioning Ratcliff about Northumberland and Surrey, who had had last night the task of going round and heartening the men. He seems reassured by this, annoyed that the morning is cloudy and the ground still damp with dew, which makes going difficult, and with every line recovering more and more of his old efficiency, hard as it may be to do it. The brisk line, 'Come, bustle, bustle, caparison my horse' introduces a series of firm, precise instructions about the order of battle, culminating in a bold defiance of anything like doubt, hesitation or hidden treachery. The rumour that he has been 'bought and sold' is contemptuously dismissed, as are the last remnants of that 'coward conscience' that had tormented him in the night-time, and the verse whirls on to its ringing, heartening conclusion

> March on, join bravely, let us to't pell-mell;
> If not to heaven, then hand in hand to hell!

The use of the rhyming couplet is interesting here. It usually marks the end of a scene, and when excited and declamatory it is a good cue to the audience for applause and relaxation, but as modern texts are printed this particular couplet occurs not only in the middle of a scene but in the middle of a speech. This is not what one might expect, but a little further consideration of the scene may show us a very good reason for it.

What is really significant is the fact that after this, Richard never has such a couplet again. He never has time for one. On the unlocalised Elizabethan stage we are not tied, by what we see, to one special place or time. This couplet makes, and marks, the last emotional break in the action, and rounds off, in effect, the penultimate scene. With the lines that follow, it is clear that the morning is further advanced, and Richard is addressing a different audience in a different way. Instead of semi-intimate conversation with his officers, he is now delivering a formal oration—in modern warfare we should call it a pep-talk—to his men before going into action. Probably Burbage would have left the group of nobles and come down to the out-thrust front of the stage, as if the playgoers before him were his own men ready for battle. Richmond has done the same in an earlier scene, laying emphasis on the fact that it is Richard, not his army, that is England's enemy; now it is Richard's turn to put his case, and he does so by a cheerful black-guarding of the opposing troops. His own followers are assured that *they* are the real, the only Englishmen, and that their opponents are a pack of ill-nourished foreigners, led by a poor relation who has lived abroad for years. It is a good speech, encouraging and inspiring, but before it can reach its full trumpet-tone (which Burbage almost certainly could not have produced anyway because he had not that sort of voice) it is interrupted by the far-off sound of the drums. The great war-machine has begun to move.

There is no more pausing after that. Four splendid lines follow, that might have come from the mouth of Henry V, then the sudden news that Stanley is refusing to bring up his troops. The automatic order to behead his son is nullified by Norfolk's cry that 'the enemy is past the marsh'. The moment of impact is upon them, and the beheading will have to wait till afterwards. Richard gives the word accordingly, and they hurry away. It is significant that his last line ends with a short-vowelled, un-resonant word ending in three consonants. 'Victory sits on our helms' is a statement, not a triumphant conclusion, and comes out hurriedly from a man already going on to something else. Even as he and his officers leave the stage, they plunge into the sound of battle. Without further pause, the spectators are given the sound of 'alarums', and perhaps the sight of a few armed figures in confused and violent action; then, keeping up the continuity, they learn from the sudden meeting of Catesby and Norfolk that the king is hard pressed, and that the day is going against him.

Here, curiously enough, a small but famous scene is apt to be deprived, through our unfamiliarity with tradition, of much that made it famous. In the scene of the arrest of Hastings, this had happened through the omission of a visual and aural stage-effect; here, more subtly, it is a matter of vocal cadence alone. When Richard comes in, battered but indomitable and shouting for a horse, the usual, and apparently obvious, reaction is for Catesby's response to be couched in terms of eager co-operation, so that the king's indignant reception of it appears both ungracious and unreasonable. What we no longer learn in our history-books, though the Elizabethans did in theirs, is that Richard's followers urged him to take flight, and actually broughr him a swift horse to bear him away, but that he scorned the idea, turned the horse about, shut down his visor and rushed back to death among his enemies. The little episode is unstageable as it stands, but so expressive, and so attractive to a dramatist as a last glimpse of Richard's best qualities, that it is obviously worth while to get it in somehow, and this is how Shakespeare does it. Catesby's one line can take on a very different meaning if the accent is laid on the first word and all that it stands for. His nerve is going, his hopes of success are gone, and he is frantically urging his master to admit as much by flight. The words '*Withdraw*, my lord; *I*'ll help you to a horse', instead of agreement can imply counter-suggestion and panic, and that is how Richard treats them. When a man fails, or hesitates, to carry out his design, Richard has no further use for him, and with that scornful, raging cry of 'Slave!' he sweeps Catesby from his mind, and probably from the stage, even as he had done, in the hour of his enthronement, with the unwisely importunate Buckingham. The two men think of that horse in diametrically opposite terms. to one, it stands for continuance of the battle, to the other, for abandonment of it, and the very tone of their voices can reflect the difference in their minds. After that first savage word, Richard may well have addressed his lines to anybody, or to nobody on a suddenly emptied stage, for now he is alone in all essentials, and there is nothing left for him but confrontation with Richmond, a terrific sword-combat, and death. Richmond's part has been kept very small and very simple, so that an actor could be cast for it on his fighting-quality above all. It is another Burbage accomplishment, and from his and the author's standpoint it is well worth while giving him a chance to display it instead of a last dying speech.

So the play ends. As a performance, it has provided a tremendous advertisement for Burbage, and as a part written for an actor-manager and part-owner of the theatre it has served, in its quiet way, as a reasonable advertisement for Shakespeare as a valuable member of the company. He never wrote another part in which Burbage had to do quite so many different things, but he would never need to. Actor and playwright obviously understood and appreciated each other, and their successful alliance was to last thenceforth for nearly 20 years.

Chapter Six

QUICK-CHANGE IN VERONA

WHAT PART, we may wonder, did Burbage play in *Romeo and Juliet,* the first tragedy Shakespeare wrote for the new management? He is given credit for having played Romeo, among other parts, in a set of memorial verses which have been attributed to John Fletcher, but which did not appear in print until the early 19th century, and then only in scraps. Extracts from the complete poem were printed by John Payne Collier in his *New Particulars Regarding the Works of Shakespeare* in 1836, and the whole of it in his *Memoirs of the Principal Actors in the Plays of Shakespeare* 10 years later. The trouble is, however, that Payne Collier's use of supposedly unpublished material has never been above suspicion. By training a lawyer, by profession a literary journalist, he was by instinct a fascinated examiner of documentary material that might throw any more light on Shakespeare and his fellows in the worlds of literature and the stage. He did much careful research, and published his results, giving great assistance to Shakespearean scholarship in his time, but it soon appeared that there was one serious flaw to be noted in his character. He could not let his conclusions rest upon the available evidence, but took to backing them up by citing 'unpublished' documents that were not only unpublished but non-existent, and at times, still more deplorably, by forging imitation Elizabethan and Jacobean manuscripts and—perhaps worst of all—writing amendments and additions into the text of real ones.

This regrettable tendency had got him into trouble when he was 30 (he misrepresented a parliamentary speech that he was officially reporting for *The Times*), and its application to Shakespearean studies was repeatedly challenged in a controversy running from 1853 to 1860. He had been

93

librarian to the Duke of Devonshire, and had added a
Shakespearean reference to one of the Inigo Jones costume-
designs in the library at Chatsworth; he had been given
access, in his capacity as a distinguished Shakespearean
scholar—which he quite unquestionably was—to the
Ellesmere papers at Bridgwater House and the Alleyn
collection at Dulwich, and had made his own gratuitous
additions to all of them. He roundly denied all these allega-
tions to the end, but when he died in 1883 his papers were
found to contain drafts for the interlined passages in
Henslowe's diary at Dulwich, and the matter was beyond
doubt.

It is difficult to conceive how a serious, dedicated scholar
could bring himself to falsify original material. One can
understand a man's backing his arguments by dogmatic
assertions, self-justified by confidence in his own supreme
authority and contempt of any contrary opinions; one can
imagine the further step of confounding the opposition
(after mentally dismissing it as ignorant and imperceptive)
by citing evidence hitherto unheard-of and in fact not in
existence, but the step of defacing original documentary
material by the addition of one's own fabrications is a fall
indeed.

We must be careful, then, how far we go in accepting
details about Burbage when they rest on the evidence of
Payne Collier alone, and it is more than doubtful whether
he played the part of Romeo at all. He was in his mid-
twenties—which to the Elizabethans meant a considerable
degree of maturity—when the play came out, and so much
of it turns on the extreme youth of the boy-and-girl lovers
that it would be a dangerous piece of casting if the balance
of the play were to be maintained. Indeed, it still is, as
many experienced actors have found to their cost. Romeo's
charm is the charm of youth; part of the drama in his
character is the change from youth to maturity forced
upon him by sudden tragedy and emotional strain, so that
when confronted by young Paris on the threshold of the
tomb he can say without self-consciousness

Good gentle youth, tempt not a desperate man.

but it is easier for a young actor to counterfeit maturity at the very end of the play than for an older one to give *and keep up* the impression of extreme youth through all that has gone before. Particularly is this so when we have seen him continually accompanied, encouraged, teased, and in the kindliest, most genial way, patronised by the somewhat older and infinitely more sophisticated Mercutio. The very name carries a suggestion of the mercurial quality of this fascinating figure, with his brilliance, badinage, flashes of bawdry, sudden savagery, and equally sudden, tragic death. One can see how it was imperative to kill him off half-way through the play, or he would have upset its balance completely. As it is, his death, with its effect on his young friend and avenger, provides the turning-point in the drama by stimulating Romeo to action and thereby, ultimately, to banishment and death.

Here, then, it would seem, was the ideal part for the experienced and versatile Burbage, if it were not so short. How effective it can be in the hands of a brilliant youth counterfeiting maturity was triumphantly demonstrated for all time by Gielgud and Olivier when they alternated the parts of Romeo and Mercutio in the days when we were young. Fifteen years later, with the width of a war between, their contemporary, Esmond Knight, was a magnificent Mercutio in another production, but would never, by that time, have been an obvious choice for Romeo. So, indeed, it may have been with Burbage. A natural Romeo can put on age and imitate the maturity of Mercutio, but an actor who has reached that maturity finds it harder to reverse the process, and the better he does it, the more does the *tour-de-force* of his performance distract the spectators, in their admiration of it, from what Shakespeare himself made Hamlet call the necessary questions of the play. It would lessen the impact, and impair the real effect of the tragedy, for in the process of admiring Burbage the spectators would be correspondingly forgetting Romeo.

The same thing might, at first, be said of Mercutio. After his death-scene—the first really tragic death-scene in the whole Shakespearean canon—the knowledge that Romeo has lost a dear and valued friend would be subconsciously

tempered and obscured by the realisation that the spectators
had seen the last of their best actor. Romeo's life, and the
life of Verona, would not be the same without Mercutio—
that was acceptable as part of the play—but the performance
would not be the same without its leading player, and there
was still half the play to go. That, from the box-office point
of view, was serious. The better the player, the greater the
risk of the audience's losing interest when he dropped out
of the play, unless there could be come indication, by that
time, that in spite of this they had not seen the last of him.
This must have been evident from the first, and the author
would have had to do something about it if the play were
to be worth putting into rehearsal at all.

What he presumably did, was suggested to the present
writer by the legend of a remark made long ago by a leading
member of Frank Benson's Shakespearean company. Benson
himself was playing Romeo, and the casting of the other
parts was being arranged when the actor said reflectively to
a colleague, 'Ye know, me boy, I can't make up me mind
whether to play Mercutio and go home early, or the Friar
and keep me trousers on'. What he overlooked was the fact
it was possible, in all seriousness, to do both, and a little
study of the two parts illustrates the ease with which a man
like Burbage could have done it.

A friar's frock and cowl will go on over practically anything. Marlowe had known as much when he made Faustus
send Mephistophilis away, immediately on his first sensational appearance, to 'go, and return an old Franciscan friar',
and both Shakespeare and Burbage would remember that.
After his nearly-riotous appearance on the way home from
the banquet—and who can forget the exuberance of Olivier
bounding across the stage in his carnival costume, shouting
ribaldry and blowing a squeaking horn?—Mercutio has the
whole balcony scene to change in. Zurbaran's painting of a
praying Franciscan, in the National Gallery (Plate II), shows
how the cowl not only shades the face, but affects, by its
characteristic outline, the whole appearance and carriage
of the head. There might or might not be time to hook on
what Iago, in a later play, was to call 'an usurp'd beard';
the audience in that theatre was used to 'doubling' and

would readily accept the fact without comment or question—
and, originally, without knowing how soon Mercutio was
to die.

The Friar's opening speech is completely different from
anything Mercutio has been heard to say. Its tranquil
couplets carry on the lyrical effect induced by the rhyming
conclusion of the scene before, and it comes as something
very like a slow movement after the recent activities. Instead
of the extremes of hate and love we have contemplation,
instead of emotion, quiet wisdom, instead of the bustle of
fight and feast, and the vigorous crowd-movements of the
preceding acts, the stage is occupied by a solitary figure
going peacefully about the labours of the day. The basket on
his arm, specified in the stage-direction of the early Quarto,
indicates at once that he is not indoors, but out in the open
air, not shopping, but gardening, or gathering wild plants
in the countryside, as men and women were often seen to
be doing on the outskirts of London. At first sight, to those
unfamiliar with the play, his reflections on plants and their
medicinal powers would appear to be no more than an
interlude of kindly, scholarly moralisation in the manner of
an Elizabethan Wordsworth, but in fact it is insidiously
building up for us an impression not only of the Friar's
character, but of his interests and technical knowledge. By
virtue of it, we are ready to accept him, later on, as an
authority on the subject of drugs and potions.

Meanwhile the calm, steadying influence of his character
has had its effect on Romeo, who falls in with his mood
and manner of speech. Their whole conversation is carried
out in rhyme, but the impression it gives is not one of jingling
line-capping and ingenuity, but rather of what one may
here call suitability, the young man deferring to the old one
and instinctively answering him in his own idiom. With his
Franciscan habit, Burbage has taken on a completely
different personality from Mercutio's, but has not, as yet,
been put to the task of developing it in full. So far, his lines
are calm and rather sententious, designed to temper Romeo's
emotion rather than to display any strong feelings of his own,
but his first real *tour-de-force* is now to come. As his young
friend is eagerly trying to hurry him away, he slows him

down with a line full of sibilants, impossible to speak with anything like speed. 'Wisely and slow', he says, 'They stumble that run fast', and with that thought of discretion and deliberation he leaves the stage. Next moment comes a quick change. His Franciscan habit is much more easily whipped off than assumed; like the Bensonian actor, he has 'kept his trousers on' and is back on the stage in doublet and hose, impulsively and imperiously crying, 'Where the devil should this Romeo be?' Time has moved up, the morning is far advanced, and Mercutio is up and about again after the activities of the night before.

The change is complete. The carefully-measured cadences of the old scholar have given place to rushing, restless prose, leaping from theme to theme bristling with puns, mockery, social criticism and genial impropriety, and as far from the elderly churchman as chalk from cheese. It is, in a way, the old Richard technique again, and the scene is so cleverly constructed that while the audience are unavoidably admiring the brilliance of the transformation they are in no danger of missing anything important in the progress of the play. By the time Romeo enters, they have got over their appreciation of Burbage and his quick-change, and are ready to accept Mercutio as Mercutio again, as if he had never been anybody else, exuberant in his good spirits and irresistibly bringing back the love-stricken Romeo into the cheerful idiocies and indecencies of high-spirited undergraduate conversation, where thought or word flashes about from one to the other and back again with the speed, accuracy and fascination of a brilliant rally on the tennis-court or exchange on the floor of a *salle d'armes*.

His final fling of cheerfully outrageous conversation with Juliet's nurse (who contrives to be highly indignant and at the same time to suggest that she is rather enjoying it) is followed by an immediate and quick departure, and once again, though we do not realise it, a little more time for his quick-change in the tiring-house while Romeo is calming the old lady down before she can get to the main business of her message. Similarly, in the next scene, her breathlessness, and the time she takes to get to the point, are cover for the change, and serve to ensure that Friar Laurence will be quite

ready, in cowl and cassock, when he is wanted for the important episode of the marriage. He has only 18 lines in it, but
he is the dominant figure, and begins and ends the scene.
Off come frock and cowl again as soon as it is over, and
Mercutio is ready to open the third act with some characteristic prose, not so flippant this time, as there is an
undercurrent of keen and sinister purpose—to find and
quarrel with Tybalt and, if possible, kill him, before he can
pick a chance to do as much for the more inexperienced
Romeo. When things turn out tragically otherwise, he has
time for his final change, and possibly for some work on his
make-up, for now that Mercutio is dead he must be Friar
Laurence to the end.

And, with that change, he develops tremendously in
character. In his first scene with Romeo he was an outside
observer, first having to be informed of the situation and
then gently though critically commenting upon it; next he
was seen giving support and co-operation by his readiness
to perform the marriage. Now, with responsibility thrust
upon him, he becomes a dominating figure, upbraiding and
consoling Romeo as circumstances require, and directing
the action instead of merely observing it. His very words
are no longer a calm procession of sententious couplets.
The opening line of the scene is a stern command, and he
speaks throughout with an authority that he has not had
occasion to show before, first breaking the news of Romeo's
banishment, then reminding him that he might very well
have been condemned to death, urging him, in growing
exasperation, to pull himself together, and finally giving him
a tongue-lashing for his hysterical despair. It is a small but
interesting point that in this scene and the scene of the
hurried, secret wedding he has used the imagery of the
firearm. First the violent ends of violent delights have been
compared to the spark and powder 'which as they kiss,
consume', now he takes the metaphor a stage further and
roundly says that accidental explosions are, as often as not,
the result of ignorance and stupidity, comparing Romeo
to a 'skill-less soldier' who has blown himself up by not
taking the proper precautions with his ammunition.
Accidents like that were not infrequent at the military

'musters' that took place from time to time in Moorfields, not far from the theatre, and both Shakespeare and his audience (largely, be it remembered, a local audience) had every reason to know it.

The treatment is effective. Romeo recovers himself and is grateful, and the Friar dismisses him, with instructions rather than advice, and with the reassurance that he himself will make arrangements to keep Romeo informed of what goes on while he is in safety in Mantua. The scene has been the Friar's throughout, and attempts to make Romeo the most important character in it are apt to upset the balance of the play by laying undue, and unwelcome, emphasis on his emotion without making it clear how, and how soon, he will recover from it.

By the opening of the fourth act, the Friar is no longer an observer and counsellor on the outside of the action. He is now drawn right into it, and emotionally affected in his turn. The sudden decision of Capulet to have Paris and Juliet married in three days' time comes as an unexpected shock, and disconcerts him considerably. Once again, the cessation of Mercutio's part has left the Friar free to develop a personality of his own, and to let the audience into the doubts, fears and anxieties that lie deeper than his usual combination of simplicity and wisdom. He is upset and at a loss, and at first can only object to Paris that this is very short notice to give for such an important step, especially as the bridegroom himself does not yet know what the bride thinks about it. The bridegroom's explanation gives him no help at all, with its calm conclusion, 'Now do you know the reason of this haste'. His muttered line of soliloquy underlines the irony of the remark, for he knows one quite incontrovertible reason against the haste, and heartily regrets his knowledge. On Juliet's entry he stands perplexed and silent throughout her little conversation with Paris, merely putting in four words of rhyming platitude in his old manner. The two young people are answering each other in courteous badinage, the boy—for he is little more—giving the girl already the title of 'wife', while she demurely puts it aside with the qualification 'may be'. He catches at this with 'That may be, must be, love, on Thursday next', and she in her turns equivocates with 'what must be, shall be', to which the Friar adds the corroboration, 'That's a certain text'. On the face of it, the remark is merely that of an old gentleman uttering the obvious, and so it would appear to Paris. To Juliet it comes as encouragement, a hint that, great as is the difficulty, there will be some way to get her out of it, while to the speaker it means perhaps the exact opposite. What must be, will be, and he has no notion what it is. Paris is all certainty and happiness; Juliet upheld only by hope and confidence in her confessor's wisdom, and the confessor himself unhappy and unsure of what may come.

More and more, the part reveals itself as a fine one for the actor, and the lines give a deeper insight into the character of the man, just as Juliet's outburst of distress, as soon as Paris has gone, shows the innate determination, and readiness to go to extremes, that had led her into her courtship at the beginning. Even though she recognised it as 'too rash, too unadvis'd, too sudden' in the very moment of its inception, she went ahead with her suggestions and encouragements for the secret marriage, and now she is prepared, in desperation, to destroy herself if the Friar can find no way out of the dilemma. It is her urgent, passionate speech that brings him back to himself, and gives him strength to consider something that may be possible after all. We have been prepared, by his very first appearance, to accept him as wise in the properties of herbs and plants, and can the more readily follow his design as it grows and takes more definite shape in the course of his speech. Once he has admitted the possibility, he sees the plan opening before him and can elaborate it with details, incidentally making it clear to the spectators that the funeral, with the body in its 'best robes uncovered on the bier', is no special arrangement to suit the course of the story, but the normal practice in Italian families of position. (It is one of the things that Fynes Moryson, that indefatigable traveller and observer, had recorded in his account of Italian life and customs at the time when the play was written.) By the time he has got to the end of his speech, his words have the true ring of confidence and encouragement, and his technical knowledge gives Juliet's heart the reassurance that her own display of strength and determination have already given to his. The scene is not merely explanatory; it is highly dramatic in its tension and its revelation of character in the old scholar and the young bride alike, and it is the pace of the words, as well as their meaning, that have done much to make it so.

The change of pace in the next scene, with old Capulet bustling round and fussing about the wedding arrangements, makes it all the more natural that he should take advantage of Juliet's new readiness to do as she is told. Before we know where we are, the date of the wedding has been advanced to the very next day. Juliet's agreement runs readily and smoothly off the tongue; impulsive as ever, she is eager for the Friar's plan to be put into operation, and gives no thought to the fact that this is now leaving him very little time to make his own arrangements about keeping Romeo informed of what is going on. Instead of joining her mother in protest against this further haste—though with all the women of his household objecting, even old Capulet might have thought better of it—she accepts it with apparently quite genuine delight, and unwittingly precipitates her own destruction. By being thus advanced, her supposed death occurs in time for Romeo's man Balthasar to have heard of it, seen the funeral and taken the news to his master before Friar Laurence could do anything to supplement his letter of explanation, so unfortunately delayed by being held in quarantine.

Meanwhile, we are shown another aspect of the Friar. When he comes in, ostensibly to bring the bride to church, his reception of the news reveals him in his professional capacity, as an ordained priest, at once taking charge of the scene and delivering to the mourners the kind of calm, grave rebuke that is itself a consolation. It is so impressive, and so moving, that it gives us a kind of shock to realise that it is all falsehood, and that the speaker knows it and is deliberately deceiving the grief-stricken household. It is one thing to enjoy the sight of a self-confessed villain like Richard of Gloucester uttering the best of sentiments from the worst of motives, but it is more painful to see a good man, respected and trusted for his goodness, exploiting that trust in support of an elaborate lie. His very success in it makes it the more embarrassing and distasteful. Played as Burbage would have been able to play it, that speech could have aroused instinctive reverence for its sanctity and, in a moment, revulsion and apprehension for its approach to something very near blasphemy. Heaven's name has been taken in vain; a design which depends on such hypocrisy cannot be allowed to succeed, and, sure enough, it does not.

An expressive stage-direction here, in the first Quarto edition of the play, runs, 'They all but the Nurse go forth, casting rosemary on her and shutting the curtains'. These would be the central hangings at the back of the stage, and Juliet's bed would have been set behind them, in the space between the hangings and the back wall of the theatre. Attention has now to be distracted from this part of the stage, where the stage-hands are busy removing the bed and preparing Juliet's tomb, with a certain amount of bumping and shuffling and bulging of the curtains. The quickest and best way of doing this is to bring on the clowns for a little brisk, crude back-chat in close proximity to the audience, whose laughter will do much, in its turn, to drown those unavoidable noises behind the scenes. It has been objected that there is nothing particularly funny in the conversation between the musicians and Peter the serving-man, but a little consideration of the technique of cross-talk comedians, as distinct from Shakespearean actors, will show that there does not need to be. It is in the delivery and reception of the remarks that the mirth lies, not in the quality of the remarks themselves. Wit is one thing, solemn absurdity is another, and it is absurdity that we need, and get, in this passage, even though, or indeed *because,* the clowns consider it to be wit, and say so. The bustling entry of Peter is enough to set the tone of the episode. A good clown knows just how to make that sort of an entry without seeming to do anything deliberate. That the Elizabethans knew it too is evident from a memorial verse to the famous clown Tarlton, claiming that the audience would begin to laugh at the very sight of him putting his head through the curtains of the tiring-house, before he had begun to speak.

It is just the same here. There is nothing esoterically witty in saying, 'I'll give you the minstrel' as if this enshrined a subtle Elizabethan joke; but with a resentful tone, and more accent on the personal pronoun, it becomes natural at once. The daughter of the house is dead, Peter the clown has just asked for a tune to cheer him up, and the minstrels have refused to play. 'Minstrels, indeed, *I'll* give you Minstrels' is surely the thought behind the line, and the minstrel retaliates in kind. The comedians have their cross-talk, the audience has its laughter, and the stage-hands have their time to get the bed out of the way, and their scene-setting over, before Romeo's next scene, where it is important that everybody should be able to hear the words and, at the same time, get the full value of words, vocal tone and, perhaps most impressive of all, silence.

Romeo's opening lines in the last act have a ring of quiet happiness, quite unexpected in a banished man separated indefinitely from his newly-married bride. Instead of anxiety, eagerness is the feeling uppermost in his greeting of his servant Balthasar, and he asks for news of Juliet in serene confidence that it will be good news. He has heard nothing of her sudden betrothal to Paris, and he is told nothing of it now. All he hears, broken to him as gently as Balthasar can do it, is that she is dead, and that Balthasar himself has seen her buried in the family tomb. The whole news, including Balthasar's attempt at respectful consolation, occupies no more than five lines, and the fifth rings like the conclusion of a speech, 'And presently took post to tell it you'. His task is done, his tale is told, and it is for him to stand silent and await his master's orders.

But there are no orders, no reply. Quite possibly, Balthasar, entering from one of the theatre doors near the back, has spoken his lines straight down-stage, so that it would be natural, even on the Elizabethan stage, for Romeo's face to be turned away from the greater part of the audience. What Balthasar sees there, we can only guess from the halting lines that follow. They are not a direct consequence of what has gone before; the feeling that prompts them is quite different, and suggests that there has been a pause of stricken silence that has grown almost unendurable, and that—however lamely—it has to be broken somehow. The little piece of apology and exculpation

> O pardon me for bringing these ill news,
> Since you did leave it as my office, sir,

tails off inconsequently into another silence, and Romeo breaks it at last with a line quietly spoken, but not spoken to Balthasar at all.

> Is it e'en so? Then I defy you, stars.

It is Romeo's turn now to turn and speak down-stage rather than look his messenger in the face. His next lines are quiet still, but incisive, almost reassuring in the fact that they are specific instructions what to do next. The near-hysterical Romeo, who claimed to be Fortune's fool and made such an exhibition of himself in the Friar's cell, has grown up, practically in a moment, and has achieved manhood at a terrible cost. He knows what he intends to do, and sees clearly enough how to do it, once he has gone over it carefully in his mind. It is that process, not mere scenic description, that is mirrored for us in the speech that follows, and we in turn follow his mind in recollection successively of the apothecary, his looks, his herb-gathering, his poverty-stricken, dingy little shop, and the instinctive feeling that this is the sort of place to which people might come for squalid back-street business like the purchase of forbidden drugs.

The sad little transaction is soon over, and Romeo goes away with a concluding couplet that makes it quite clear not only what he going to do, but where he is going to do it. This gives an added irony to the next scene, in which the Friar learns that his messenger has been delayed. His feeling is one of irritation rather than alarm, since for all he knows, no message has gone to Romeo at all, and the young man will be still at Mantua, waiting for news and instructions. It is only a matter of delay, not the embarrassment of having to conceal a young woman in his own cell, that his words indicate, and another letter to Romeo should put matters right. Once again, this all becomes much more important, and more exciting, if the Friar is played by someone who is a leading actor of the first rank, and is known to be such. The spectators will the more readily concentrate on him and feel interest in his individual reactions, while with a minor player, however skilful, to follow his mind too closely would seem to be an irrelevant digression from the main story. But in point of fact Friar Laurence *is* by this time an integral part of the main story, and will remain so till the end.

With the beginning of the last scene, Shakespeare has at once called upon the words to do his stage-lighting for him. The sight and mention of the torch indicate in the first line that it is night; the instruction to 'put it out, for I would not be seen', reminds us that the stage is meant to be in darkness, but at the same time the uncompromising Elizabethan daylight will still serve to make it quite clear what Paris is doing and, from the sight of his expression, what he is feeling, as he decks the tomb with flowers and speaks a quatrain and couplet that would seem to be the opening of a funeral elegy, interrupted next moment by his page's signal. He withdraws, with a final reminder that he is covered by the imaginary darkness, and the stage is clear for the appearance of Romeo, whose purpose is quite determined, though even now he has not told Balthasar what he means to do, covering his true intent by an untrue story about a ring. Even so, Balthasar is not entirely convinced, and does not go very far away.

Romeo's sudden maturity is made quite clear when he is interrupted by the indignant Paris. Hitherto they have been seen to be more or less contemporaries, with Paris, perhaps, a little the elder and more sophisticated of the two, but now Romeo's gentle remonstrance has the ring of sudden, immeasurable seniority in the antithesis of 'youth' with 'desperate man'. There might be a generation or more between them as he gives the young man wise, sad counsel from one who is about to die, and knows it. The old 'self—self' echo, familiar from *Titus Andronicus* and *Richard III*, has here acquired a sort of wry kindliness, ending in a couplet of dismissal that seems to come from an infinite distance,

> Stay not, be gone, live, and hereafter say
> A madman's mercy bade thee run away.

But the plea is fruitless, Romeo is stung by its rejection, and instead of 'gentle youth', his opponent becomes 'boy'—a particularly insulting term among the Elizabethans. The swords are out, they cross, and in a moment Romeo is once more standing over a dead or dying man. The shock of realisation changes his mood completely, and the tone of his voice with it. His singleness of purpose and concentration upon his one object are suddenly gone, and he stands reflective and uncertain, trying to remember what his man told him on the road from Mantua, and filled with increasing pity for the man he has killed, and even, in a few moments, for his other victim, Tybalt, who lies in the vault already. It is the sight of the dead Juliet that steadies him and brings him to a mood of contemplation, tranquility and contentment that sustains him through the little life that he still has to live.

It has been said before now that this play marks a stage in its author's progress in that Mercutio's is the first really tragic death-scene that Shakespeare wrote. Looking at the play, and listening to it, *as a whole,* we may perhaps claim something more, on the strength of this final speech and its revelation not so much of Romeo's character as of his state of mind. Hitherto he has been controlled by a series of more or less violent emotions, expressing themselves now in impatience, now in sheer beauty, now again in schoolboy wit, savagery or hysteria, but at this last point all those passions are behind him; he can, as it were, step back out of himself and look at himself, without resentment, as one already dead. This state of calm, the restfulness of a mind that has gone beyond the disturbing influence of earthly hopes, is a thing we meet occasionally in the later plays, but we are not always ready to recognise it here. Brutus, when the battle is lost and his friends are already dead, reflecting thankfully on the friendship and loyalty he has found throughout his life, Hamlet, in the little scene after Osric's departure, reassuring Horatio that 'the readiness is all', Cleopatra preparing herself 'again for Cydnus' and resolutely leaving her womanly qualities to baser life, are all familiar to us, but it is interesting, and revealing, to see how this quality is to be noticed in the less familiar plays. Timon, having lost one fortune, found another one and disdained it, comes to think of health and life as a 'long sickness' from which he is recovering, and looks forward to the Nothing that is to bring him all things. Buckingham, in *Henry VIII*, has defended himself at his trial with what an onlooker calls 'many sharp reasons to defeat the law', he has spoken 'much and learnedly' after the verdict and uttered one sharp, angry outburst when brought to hear his sentence, but when we see him coming away from the court, all his arguments, efforts and indignation are things of the past, and he is almost glad of it, for, though desperately tired, he can say of the king

> Commend me to his grace,
> And if he speak of Buckingham, pray tell him
> You met him half in heaven:

Wolsey, his great adversary, comes in his turn to know a tremendous reversal of fortune, but after the climax of it, when he knows himself to be disgraced, discredited, stripped of all offices and honours and within appreciable danger of the executioner's axe, he can feel within himself 'a peace beyond all earthly dignities', and give wise, quiet counsel to his faithful servant. Even so, at this early stage in Shakespeare's career, it is with Romeo, making his arrangements for death and carrying them out with what a later poet was to describe as 'all calm of mind, all passion spent'.

Both the boy who played Juliet and the young man who played Romeo had been well treated by the dramatist. Each had been given one long speech in which he had the stage to himself and could use his talents to the full, without fear of interruption. If the play were about their love-story alone, it could end with Juliet's suicide, and in a good many productions between Shakespeare's time and our own, it did. But the author's theme was a larger one than that. He needed to show the audience the end of the ancient, senseless hate that had thrown three great houses into mourning, and old Montague, Capulet and the Prince must be brought together for a final confrontation at the very gates of the tomb.

Subtly and imperceptibly, this is made to turn upon the Friar. At his very first entrance he sounds breathless and uncertain, stumbling in the darkness among the graves— both the graves and the darkness are brilliantly conjured up for us by that sudden reminder on the empty stage—and desperately afraid he may be late for Juliet's awakening. In quick succession he is alarmed at finding somebody in the churchyard and relieved to see that it is only Romeo's servant, upon whom he can rely. He tries to call on him for help in the enterprise, but the man is afraid of disobeying his master's orders, so Friar Laurence has to pluck up his courage and go to the vault alone. It is the succession of his emotions and discoveries that keeps up the tension here; not merely what he finds, but what he feels, and how these feelings are going to affect his actions. The light burning in the monument has first aroused his apprehensions; then he sees the blood on the threshold and the abandoned swords, and in the tomb itself not only Romeo, but the unexpected Paris, obviously dead by violence. In contrast to all this is the still figure of Juliet on her bier, peaceful and beautiful among all this horror, but at this moment, for a culmination of horror, the body begins to move, and becomes again the living Juliet, radiant with life and, most terrible of all, with happiness. In only three lines it is made clear that the first thing she sees is the Friar, that she is overjoyed to see him (how much rapture and welcome can be got into that one word 'comfortable!') and childishly pleased to find, and to show him, that she is not bewildered nor frightened by the place in which she finds herself. Her fears when she drank the potion are groundless, she remembers the plan and is quite ready for the next stage of it, which is the arrival of Romeo, so her first question is, naturally, to ask for him, and that, unfortunately, is more than Friar Laurence can bear.

The custom of having actresses, instead of boys, to play the women's parts has altered the balance of this scene. Almost unavoidably, the leading lady takes precedence, in the matter of interest, over the supporting player, and it is on her, and her emotions, that we instinctively concentrate, but when Juliet was played by a talented boy, and the Friar by an experienced man—particularly if, as suggested, he was the leading actor and part manager of the theatre— the position must have been rather different. Juliet's actions and feelings are important, but still more important is their effect on the man who planned her sleep and her awakening, and her childlike pleasure that everything is going right intensifies the awful realisation that everything, on the contrary, is going very, very wrong.

On top of this, he can hear the sound of people approaching them through the darkness. His endorsement of her earlier 'What must be shall be' and his facile condolences to the bereaved family about the unalterable will of Heaven, are being proved true in a more awful sense that he has imagined. It is fear, rather than Christian resignation, that inspires the words

> A greater power than we can contradict
> Hath thwarted our intents, come, come away.

The noise is growing louder, discovery is imminent and his nerve breaks. One hurried appeal to her to come and let him find refuge for her in a nunnery, and he can stand it no longer, but rushes wildly away, abandoning his charge—and the audience, in those days of compulsory church-going, might well think instinctively of another crowd with lights and weapons coming into a garden, and the terse comment of the Evangelist, 'And they all forsook him, and fled'.

It is not surprising that he blunders straight into the arms of the Watch, and that he 'trembles, sighs and weeps' when taken into custody. At first one would think that everything was over for him, but in a few moments it is clear that Capulet, Montague and the Prince are drawing the wrong conclusions from what the see. With Paris dead, and Juliet dead by Romeo's dagger, it looks, on the fact of it, as if the banished Montague had come back by night and killed his enemy's daughter and her betrothed, possibly with the Friar's connivance. The bodies are hidden from sight by the closing of the tomb, and he gathers strength as he corrects fallacy after fallacy, speaking as he does with the authority of personal knowledge. Told as a mere bleating relation of events, the speech appears redundant, and is too often cut; but it is surely intended to be seen *and heard* as a correction of tragically wrong impressions.

First come three flat statements of fact. It was not a continuation of the family feud; the two young people were man and wife. It was not a passionate murder by a jealous or injured husband; Juliet was a faithful wife, to her last breath. This is not mere hearsay; the words come uncompromisingly from the lips of one who is priest and friar, 'I married them'. After that, the explanation comes, as it should, without hearsay, but confined to the speaker's own personal knowledge and actions up to the bitter moment of Juliet's death by her own hand. This he did not see; self-destruction is a grave sin of which he will not accuse her, so here, and here only, he puts in the qualifying little 'as it seems'. For the rest, he endorses his narrative with those four impressive monosyllables, 'All this I *know*,' and finally cites the Nurse as a corroborative witness to part of the story before he submits himself unquestioning to the judgement of the law.

Spoken with the requisite authority and conviction, the speech sets the tone for the Prince's answer. The line 'We still have known thee for a holy man' can sound almost fatuous if delivered as a vague comment on the story, but spoken in the same key as the story itself, it is very different. It is the Prince's grave, considered acceptance of the Friar's evidence, on the strength of his character, and leads to the supporting evidence of Romeo's man, the Count's page, and the farewell letter sent by Romeo to his father. There is no need for him to command a reconciliation; it is from Capulet that the words and gesture come. From being a testy, bustling, comic figure he has momentarily become a tragic one, and the London pleasure-seekers of the early 1590s would know better than to see any incongruity in this. Outbreaks of plague had been familiar hazards in the past few years, and many a prosperous London merchant, however self-important and absurd in his ordinary life, had been seen sobered by bereavement, or himself invested with the dignity of death. The Friar's own verbal dignity, also, cannot be ignored. It is not three stricken men, but four, who stand over the tomb of the dead lovers, and we may be justified in the assumption that the company's leading player was almost certainly one of them.

Chapter Seven

RHYME, AND THE REASON FOR IT

THE DANCING ballad-rhythms of *Love's Labour's Lost* make their appearance again in the more frivolous of the early plays attributable to Shakespeare's association with the Burbage management. *The Taming of the Shrew* is a re-written version of a rather crude old play with a good part for the leading man (a part giving scope for Richard's skill in rapid changes of mood, particularly when the play is produced in a spirit of high comedy rather than the somewhat gross buffoonery that obscured its better qualities in the 18th and 19th centuries), and *The Comedy of Errors* is a bustling and very funny farce about two pairs of twins. This is ingeniously blended with a story of old partings and misfortunes, present condemnation and ultimate recognitions and reunion of a family after a lifetime of separation. A sonorous opening couplet presents us with an old man gravely accepting a sentence of death and almost welcoming it after a series of bitter disappointments, which are revealed to us, at the judge's request, in a long and moving narrative of exposition. From this unlikely beginning springs a complicated story of mistaken identities, in verse that heightens a situation by rushing into rhyme and dance-rhythm like a first-act finale in an opera by Donizetti or Rossini, and in both this play and *The Taming of the Shrew* a final scene of some tension and considerable poetry is resolved by a change into a lilting, rhyming conclusion that suggests that the actors are literally dancing off the stage to the accompaniment of the spectators' laughter and applause.

More subtle than these variations of rhyme and metre is another characteristic that may be observed in these two plays and in a comedy that closely follows them, *A Midsummer Night's Dream*. It is the differentiation between the two leading female parts. Some may claim to have found traces of it in *The Two Gentlemen of Verona*, but it is with the others that it really comes into its own. One of the ladies—Adriana, Bianca, Helena— is the embodiment or injured innocence, and clearly sees herself as such; the other is quicker in the uptake, more extravagant and unrestrained in speech and, in the *Dream* at any rate, physically smaller and more active. The injured and innocent lady really *is* injured and innocent, and pleads for understanding and sympathy in passages of real beauty, but at the same time the very fact that she is so sorry for herself, and calls upon other people for their commiseration, makes her protestations appear excessive and her general appearance rather ridiculous. The other is quite different, in sentiments, in vocabulary and in speed of diction. In moments of tranquility she is distinctly frivolous; touch her more nearly and she becomes a little spitfire, claws out like an infuriated kitten. Herein, perhaps, lies the secret of *The Taming of the Shrew*. An Amazonian Katherina, looking and sounding like a blend of Brünnhilde and the Widow Twankey, can very easily give the play an unpleasant taste by throwing too much emphasis on the physical aspect of the contest between her and Petruchio. If, however, she were played (as she very likely was) by the boy who would later be cast for Hermia, her sparring-matches would be those of a kitten with an imperturbable St. Bernard dog, and her long speech of womanly duty at the end would become an example of the smallest kitten's ability to assume, at will, complete, self-justified command of any situation.

But the next major play, and one in which the sound as well as the sense is particularly significant, is *Richard II*. Here we have history again, but history with a difference. Comparisons are obvious, with Marlowe's *Edward II* on the one hand and Shakespeare's own *Henry VI* plays on the other, and it can be easily seen how Shakespeare's handling of this new subject, particularly from the vocal angle, has enhanced the best qualities of both. The story of Richard is used as Hall used it, not only for the pathos of his fall and sufferings, but for its importance as the starting-point of the rise of the house of Lancaster, the other plays having

already chronicled its fall. Taken together, the two tetra-
logies cover practically all the period, *and the theme,* of
Hall's *Chronicle,* with the story of Henry VIII, the most
active and terrible of the Tudor sovereigns, coming along
at a safe distance, when the last of the Tudor line was dead.

In form, the play offers the greatest possible contrast
to the earlier histories in the sequence. There are no combats
on the battlefield, no sensational sound-effects with off-stage
cannon, like those at Orleans and Auvergne, no half-comic,
half-terrible figures like Cade and his rabble, or the murderers
of the duke of Clarence. We might almost say that there
were no sudden surprises, like the arrest of Hastings at the
council-board, and no acts of violence of any kind, were we
not suddenly confronted with them in the penultimate scene
of all. Yet the play had, and retains, the power to interest
and move an audience, and setting aside for the moment
any dutiful feelings that we have got to respect it because
it is History, and to admire it because it is Shakespeare,
we may justifiably make a little effort to find out why.

Consideration of *Love's Labour's Lost* may very well
help us on the way to an answer, though the ultimate
answer is one that each individual reader or spectator must
decide for himself, in the light of his own personal reactions.
As in that comedy, so in this history, the first approach
is made through the ear, rather than the eye, and directed at
the mind, not at the emotions. At the time of its composition
and first production, there was a closer resemblance than one
might always realise between the court life of Richard's
day and that of the late 16th century. It was an age of
appreciation and enjoyment, of extreme formality coupled
with a strong feeling for poetry and beauty in all forms of
social life, of pageantry and what the poet was later to
describe as 'silken dalliance' combined with genuine feats
of arms. And, underlying all this stately artificiality, there
were still the ordinary human passions and emotions and
antagonisms, working themselves out in their own way,
sometimes in conformity with current custom, sometimes
in shocking and abrupt contrast. Much that was shown as
happening at Richard's court could very well happen at
Elizabeth's. That made the play easily understandable and

natural-seeming when it was first put on. People took the
various emotions and reactions for granted as natural and
universal, without consciously realising the resemblance.
When they eventually *did* realise it, and began to apply it
and draw comparisons on their own account, it held a different interest for them, and when in due course the queen
realised it, there was trouble.

Figure 4.—Two of the various figures used indiscriminately by Holinshed several times over to represent early kings, showing the dignity
and authority that the Elizabethans were ready to ascribe to monarchs
in general, especially those of legendary and historic times.

At the outset, however, this resemblance merely led the
audience to understand and accept the situations, not to
draw political parallels, and here as elsewhere the relation
of the characters is established and maintained by the very
sound, as well as the sense, of the words they use, and that
others use about them. In the very first word of the first
line the audience is prepared for a point that is dramatically
necessary but historically incorrect. At the time of the
Mowbray-Bolingbroke quarrel, with which the play opens,
the king's uncle, John of Gaunt, was a man in his late
fifties, an ably-scheming but usually unsuccessful place-
hunter and politician. For dramatic purposes, however, he
needs to be presented in a rather more favourable light, as
the head of the house of Lancaster and grandfather of the

future Henry V. Shakespeare has accordingly turned him into a venerable and patriarchal figure, typifying the old order of things, one of the last survivors of the age of chivalry, and a worthy brother of the Black Prince. That is how audiences are to regard him, and the king's opening words incline them unwittingly to do it. It is almost impossible, and certainly unnatural, to hurry over or throw away a line like

Old John of Gaunt, time-honoured Lancaster,

with its long vowels that make for resonance, and double consonants that slow down the pace and give it dignity and meaning. That line, and the two or three that follow it, call for the vocal organ-notes that most actors can assume for certain selected moments only, though it takes an Alleyn or a John Philip Kemble to keep them up for the whole of the play. Richard has no need to do as much as that, and does not. His anxious questions to his uncle seem to go at a quicker pace and rather a different pitch, expressive of the apprehensions that lie behind them, and a couplet of soliloquy, when Gaunt has gone to bring his son into the Presence, indicates how little liking he has for the interview that is to come.

When it comes, it is almost operatic in its word-music, the altercation between Bolingbroke and Mowbray ringing out like a Verdi duet between tenor and baritone. Bolingbroke is passionate in his attack; Mowbray dignified and unflinching in his resistance to it. Bolingbroke, at the height of his passion, breaks into rhymed couplets, where Mowbray, in his defence, uses them only to round off a speech, and Richard's couplets which follow have in their turn a completely different sound. They are placidly sententious, making little of the matter by their very formality, and couplets continue practically to the end of the scene. The result is that, as with a musical setting, the most passionate expressions come out under some degree of control, and conform to certain well-established requirements, keeping the impression that the quarrel is taking place in a civilised court, and in the presence of a king. When it threatens to get out of hand, a whip-crack of a line from Richard brings

it up short; then come three non-rhyming lines giving instructions to the adversaries and information to the audience, and
with three more rhyming couplets formality returns, the
scene closes and the situation is in hand again. And, what is
more, uncertain and untrustworthy as he is, it is the king
whose incisiveness and authority have made it so.

The following scene gives the intending combatants time
to change, or at least to get out of the enveloping gowns
which, in the first scene, have served to conceal their armour,
but quite apart from this practical service, it has a virtue of
its own, in bringing home to the audience something of the
consequences of Gloucester's murder, about which we have
heard so much at the beginning of the play, and are to hear
more, at an unexpected point, before the end. One word in
it has had its effect lessened by the passage of time, to a
degree which may be held to call for the normally undesir-
able practice of substituting a synonym for the word the
author actually wrote. The personal name of the murdered
duke of Gloucester was Thomas of Woodstock, and Shakespearean playgoers had a better chance of knowing it. After
all, they were living only 200 years after his time, with nearly
400 years less of English history to learn. If John of Gaunt
substitutes 'Gloucester's' for 'Woodstock's' in the opening
line of the scene, the audience will be able to understand
what he is talking about, and to identify the lady in mourn-
-ing who shares the scene with him.

This time it is her lines that set the tempo throughout.
First they ring with a note of reproach, indicative of the
'exclaims' that must have gone before; then, with the
metaphors of vials and branches, comes a passage of reminis-
cent and poetic tenderness, only to be cut short by the
sudden consonants of 'murder's bloody axe'. The music
changes to a grave reminder, and a warning of what may
come if Gaunt stays inactive for too long. If he will not
move to avenge his brother's death, he might at least do
something to avoid his own. This plea fails in its turn, and her
last hope goes with it. She has tried every argument she
knows, and can think of no other champion to summon to
her cause. After all the rhetoric, the poetry and the exhortation she is reduced to one simple, straightforward question,

'Where, then, alas, may I complain myself?' and she meets Gaunt's reply with four words of acquiescence and complete surrender. There is no more fight left in her, she is old, and disillusioned, and desperately tired, and has to pause and collect her thoughts before she can even bid her disappointing brother-in-law farewell. The thought of the impending trial by battle spurs her to a final, almost automatic imprecation on Mowbray, and the rhymed passage that concludes the scene fulfils the function of the 'slow music' that a later century would have prescribed for such an exit. In broken accents she tries to frame some message for her other brother-in-law, York, and fails, and in her very last couplet the repetition of a word, and the alliteration first of dentals and then of labials, combine to underline her utter loneliness and exhaustion as she takes her leave of the kinsman who has failed her, and whom she will never see again.

Next moment we find ourselves in a different world. The brisk exchange of question and answer between the Marshal and Aumerle show us two new characters, tells us the name of one of them and indicates the imminent arrival of three whom we have seen already. Partly by alliteration, partly by the choice of words, their placing and their sound, we are transported to the very threshold of the lists, as the opening query, 'My lord Aumerle, is Harry Hereford armed?' is roundly answered, 'Yes, at all points, and longs to enter in', and the succeeding lines ring with reference to the summons of a trumpet, and to champions prepared, eager and waiting only for the approach of the king. Two people have come in, and spoken only six lines between them, and the atmosphere is completely changed. Instead of a house of mourning, and a desolate widow dedicating herself to death because nothing can be done to right her wrongs, we are in a very different place, among sounds of hurry and bustle and the ring of arms, where something is very shortly going to be done, and two very important people are eagerly waiting for the chance to do it.

There is no delay. Trumpet answers trumpet, and the stage fills in rapid succession with the king and his court, Mowbray the defendant, and Bolingbroke the appellant, both of them in full armour and deadly serious in contrast with the fashionable civilian crowd around them. With his first words, Richard presents another facet of his character, and we can see, after a little scrutiny, how ingeniously Shakespeare has cut the part to Burbage's measure, once more giving him scope to display his infinite variety and versatility. This Richard is a man of almost as many moods and changes as Richard III, with the great difference that they are not part of deliberate policy, but natural, instinctive and unconscious, reflecting the circumstances and emotions that inspired them. His formal lines to the Marshal, the Marshal's charges to the combatants, and their several replies, are all measured and slightly archaic, clearly following a prescribed ritual, and their formality brings home the fact that, social event or not, this is a serious occasion, and is being taken seriously by those most concerned. Maurice Evans, when playing the part in 1934, spoke this opening in tones of deliberate boredom, lounging cross-legged in his chair as if contemptuous of the whole ceremony and of the words he had to speak, and this was theatrically effective for the moment but was soon forgotten in the dramatic concentration of the other three—Marshal, defendant, and appellant—on their formal interrogations and responses.

The use and avoidance of rhyme is interesting here. There is none in the speeches that are obviously part of an established ritual, but as soon as the king comes down from his chair of state to take a personal leave of his cousin, their exchanges take on, once again, the stateliness of formal verse, with rhyme answering decorously to rhyme, and confirming the impression given us in the opening scene, of personal emotion properly subjected to control. The sentiments expressed in rhymed couplets are sentiments which the speaker intends everybody to hear. They are *public* utterances, and are meant to be so, and for that purpose a certain care and artificiality have gone to their making. Bolingbroke has a cheering couplet when he takes leave of Aumerle, and a respectful, complimentary one, suitable for all to hear, when he goes last of all to greet his father, but his succeeding speech, when he asks that father for his prayers, has no such elegant ornament. It is quite personal and quite private, it comes straight from the heart and concerns

nobody but the two of them, so it is couched in the straightforward blank verse that is the ordinary medium of the play.

This general principle is consistently observed throughout.
Gaunt's answering benediction is heartfelt and unrhymed.
So—and this is particularly significant—are the lines in which
Mowbray assures the king that, whatever happens in the
combat, he himself will be loyal to his sovereign, and bear
him no ill-will for the trial he is about to undergo. Next
moment he is addressing his king, his friends and his enemy
in a burst of good will, and in terms that all are welcome to
hear, and once again the change is marked by a deliberate
return to poetic form. The king's acknowledgement is a
formal couplet, as formal and artificial as the compliment
it expresses, and thereafter the scene has done with such
things and concentrates on tension and a certain amount
of action. A fight on horseback between men in full armour
would be impossible to recreate effectively on the stage in
Shakespeare's day and our own alike, and any audience must
know as much; yet the author manages to dull that knowledge in our minds by working on the formality that has
impressed us at the very opening of the scene, and heightening the tension by a return to the ceremonies ordained for a
trial by combat.

The appellant and defendant are given their lances, each
one is duly named and presented by his personal herald,
and at last the Marshal gives the word for the starting-signal
to be sounded. The ritual of the lists has played its part so
well in building up the excitement that we really feel a sense
of shock and frustration when the sounding of the charge
is immediately followed by the command to stop, as the
king has thrown down his ward-staff, a gesture as definitive
and unmistakable as the whistle of a football referee. It is
something more than a mere false start, or one of the combatants being sent back for being too quickly off the mark;
word is given that they are both to lay aside their helmets
and lances and wait for the results of a further discussion.

Here, perhaps, the unlocalised Elizabethan stage made for
a smoother, clearer and more intimate production. Mowbray
and Bolingbroke, with their heralds and squires, have left
the stage to go back to their chairs at the opposite ends of

the lists. Richard has told Gaunt and his own company to 'withdraw with Us' and the theatre trumpeters are now sounding 'a long flourish' on the otherwise empty stage. There is nothing visible to remind the audience of the impending combat; the lists have had their part in the situation and there is no need to think of them again. Instead, an item by the threatre band serves to indicate the passage of time—some two hours, according to the chroniclers—and when their contribution ends with a fanfare for the return of the king, that passage of music, unaccompanied by words or action, has led the audience to the next situation-scene, two hours later in time and quite possibly somewhere different in place. The strength of this next scene is lessened, not heightened, when it is played against a background of blue sky and banners and open air, with their suggestion of fashionable elegance and popular festivity in the height of the season, like Henley on a fine day. The king's decision, we are told, was duly inscribed 'in a long roll' and read out to the public by Bushy, but that is not what is being set before us here. This scene shows it being communicated beforehand, as it might be in a committeeroom behind the royal box, to those immediately concerned, and shows, too, in equal privacy, their reception of it.

The king's speech has none of the heroic couplets associated with his public utterances, making them sound like incontrovertible, unquestionable truth. On the contrary, it is a grave exposition of the factors that have had to be considered by the king in council—he loses no time in mentioning the council and thereby shedding the load of his own responsibility—passing from exposition to explanation, and from explanation to excuse, for his decision, when it comes out at last, is very hard to excuse or to explain away. To avoid the risk of having the truth come out as a result of the trial, a fear that has haunted him from the very opening of the play, he tries to suppress it by banishing both parties, which is manifestly unfair, but should at least prevent Bolingbroke from discovering, and Mowbray from disclosing, the truth about Gloucester's murder and Richard's own part in it. To make himself yet safer he exacts from an oath which will effectually prevent them from meeting each other and comparing notes.

Bolingbroke's acknowledgement of the sentence is cold, proper and non-committal, and is accordingly in rhymed form that shows he has his emotions well under control. Mowbray's, when it comes, is straight from the heart, and directed to Richard personally, as from man to man. The couplet at the end serves merely to round off the speech: Richard's answer, by contrast, is a couplet of the public-utterance kind—the sort of unexceptionable truism that might quite safely be reported afterwards in the Press, but is more likely to be considered not worth mentioning. Mowbray accepts the black injustice without further protest, answering with a couplet in the same key, and the sorry business is very nearly ended. There is a subtle contrast, perhaps a deliberately ironic one, between the two champions in their reception of the final sentence. Each has had a short, powerful, unrhymed speech to the other, full of personal feeling; now Mowbray, banished unjustly from the country he has loved and served so long, puts a gallant face on the matter and goes out with the words of a knight-errant on his lips. To Bolingbroke, on the other hand, the matter appears in a different light. The immediate remission of four years of his sentence (which really happened some weeks later) calls up a realisation of the power and the waywardness of kings, and his comment, with its concluding couplet, is not so much an expression of thanks to his sovereign as an ominous indication of the course of his own mind. It is the beginning of a long silence that can be tremendously impressive on the stage, as all must know who remember the brooding eyes of Abraham Sofaer in the part as he stood absolutely motionless, wrapped in his own dark thoughts and apparently seeing nothing of the friends who came up in succession to take their leave.

It is John of Gaunt who has to cover up this apparent disregard by addressing the king himself, and his words are calculated to intensify the impression of great age, not only by their subject but once again by their very sound. The first three lines are grave and unhurried, but after that there comes a series of long vowels and double consonants that slow down the pace yet further and invest it with an oracular solemnity. The change to rhyme here seems quite natural and appropriate, the last beats of a great machine running slowly to a standstill in an almost entirely mono-syllabic line,

> My inch of taper will be burnt and done,
> And blindfold death not let me see my son.

Richard has a line of protest, but Gaunt caps it at once with an echoing answer, and the couplets that follow come out like the pronouncements of an old prophet speaking oracles. It is only this, and the continuance of the oracular tone, that can persuade us to accept such a couplet as

> You urge me as a judge, but I had rather
> You would have bid me argue like a father.

Any slackening of the tension or the tone, and the lines become archly absurd, like the satiric couplets of Planché or 'Monk' Lewis, but in their place, and after all that has gone before, they pass without incongruity.

After that speech, the king, Aumerle and the Marshal take their leave with rhyming politeness, and the relapse to passionate, emotional verse is all the more striking when Gaunt is left alone with his son. Rhyme reverts to its old function of rounding off a speech and bringing it back from emotion to formality at the end, and in the next scene there is no rhyme at all. It is one of brisk, natural conversation, suggesting once again a change of place and time, and telling the spectator something about recent and future events and a good deal more about the characters of the people who describe them. The last half-dozen lines look as if they had been written to give Burbage a chance to repeat his old *tour de force* of swift and unctuous duplicity, for behind Richard II for a moment lurks the wry-mouthed shade of that other Richard with whom he had really made his name. When Bushy comes in with the news of Gaunt's sudden illness, the king's reaction is quite unexceptionable—for a line and a half.

> Now put it, God, in the physician's mind
> To help him—

We cannot tell, and must leave it to the actor and producer to decide, whether the next four words 'to his grave immediately', and the two lines that follow, are to be spoken to the company in general, to Aumerle, or to Green—who has just mentioned the need for quick action against the Irish and might well be told at once how they can raise the money for it—or even directly to the audience as an expression of Richard's private thoughts. Next moment he does the same thing again, with an outward appeal full of apparent kindliness

> Come, gentlemen, let's all go visit him.
> Pray God we may make haste,

and a last cynical tag 'and come too late' which is all the more pungent if it is *not* heard by all the king's followers and flatterers as they leave the stage.

This reminder of an ulterior motive in Richard's visit to his uncle is more important than it looks. The next scene is only too easily regarded as entirely John of Gaunt's, through the nobility and sonority of his great dying panegyric upon England, and audiences are tempted to abandon themselves to enjoyment of the sound without giving full attention to the sense. For it is in fact full not only of poetry but of drama. With his very first words the dying man shows how he intends the inverview to go. The slow, monosyllabic opening line, the music of the couplets and the quatrain with which he continues, all suggest that his age, his earnestness and the very circumstances of the situation must carry more weight than the king's natural instincts, and even at this last moment restrain him from his unwisdom and irresponsibility. He himself is convinced of it, or very nearly so, and does his best to persuade his brother York that it is still possible to make Richard see reason at the last minute. The 'rash fierce blaze of riot' has not yet irretrievably damaged England, and when it has burnt itself out there is still a chance for the country's recovery, if the young man can be persuaded to take it. What he cannot bring himself to believe, though York repeatedly tries to tell him so, is that the king will not be in the mood to listen, as he has gone too far already.

We can see, from this text, why managements were deliberately reluctant to let their current successes get into print. When a play has been designed to make its impression by the immediate impact of sight and sound upon the spectators, that impact is weakened, and the impression lessened, if those spectators are pre-conditioned for it by having read the text beforehand. It has been said of this play that it is one in which the poetry outweighs the drama, but this is not quite accurate as a summing-up of the position. To change the metaphor from the scales to the race-track, the poetry is apt to lead because we give it an unfair start. It is not the poetry itself, but our foreknowledge of the poetry, and our instinctive concentration upon it, that can so easily distract our attention from the ordinary course of the play. We have read, or heard, this or that passage that particularly impressed us, we wait eagerly to hear it again, and while we are waiting we have only half an ear for other matters that are really worthy of attention for the sake of the plot. To the original audience, the people whom Shakespeare had to attract and interest at the first instance, if his play were to be a success, the prospect of Gaunt's great speech meant less, because they did not know it, and Richard's attitude to his uncle meant more, because they had just seen it. Richard is coming to that death-bed with a keen eye to his uncle's estate and a firm decision how to use the property when he gets it. The Elizabethan audience got its impression from its recollections of history and its observation of the play as it went on, whereas we get ours instinctively from Shakespeare, and our foreknowledge of whatever play is in question, and therein lies all the difference in the world.

That difference is made all the clearer by the sound of the words. In spite of the sonorous organ-music of Gaunt's opening lines, the little conversation-scene that has preceded them suggests very strongly that the coming interview is not going to be played in Gaunt's way, and that York is quite justified in thinking so. Richard's greeting is light, cheerful and conversational, full of consonants and short vowels and making the greatest possible contrast, in sound and spirit, to the solemn address with which the whole play began. Gaunt persists in his grave and unsparing exhortation, but Richard is in no mood now for regarding his uncle as 'time-honoured Lancaster'. He repeatedly interrupts with short, incisive lines, first of questioning and then of flat contradiction, and finally he loses his temper and abuses the dying man to his face, admitting that this 'frozen admonition' has gone home and has seriously upset him. When Gaunt has ended his last speech with two formal couplets, and has been carried out to die, Richard tries to get the last word by shouting after him an angry couplet echoing his concluding rhyme, and when York tries to smooth matters over by an apology and reassurance, he replies with another couplet, literally agreeing, but at the same time giving the words an underlying and disagreeable meaning. As in the first scene, the use of rhyme serves to give some shape of decorum to an unpleasant remark.

As soon as he hears that Gaunt is really and satisfactorily dead, Richard recovers his temper, abandons rhyme after a polite, sententious couplet, and goes on to the business he has really come for. He seems genuinely surprised by York's disapproval, and brings in rhyme again to give brevity and finality to his decision. He puts aside his uncle's protest and disregards his warning, without heat or open defiance, and on York's retirement he goes at once to the point, giving instructions and outlining his plans—which include using Ely House, the dead man's palace, as his own headquarters for the next day or two—and at the same time paying tribute to York's loyalty and integrity by putting the government of England into his hands during his own absence in Ireland. It is a chance for the actor to show another and more sympathetic facet of Richard's complex character, and the versatile Burbage was the man to take it.

At this point, we may conjecture, occurred the act-interval that has been mistakenly transferred to the end of the scene before. That earlier scene, with its first mention of the Irish troubles and Richard's plans for raising money, leads without delay to Gaunt's protests and death scene, which has left Richard able to proceed with arrangements for a punitive expedition. This is the point at which the audience should be given a moment or two in which to draw breath, reflect on what has gone before, and wonder—in the days when this was a new play—what the players were going to show them next. As with the beginning of the scene at Coventry, the opening lines are in a totally different place, a different time and a very different situation, and it is surely in error that the former scene, instead of this one, has been made to mark the beginning of a new act. The first chapter of the story ends, dramatically speaking, with Gaunt's death and the king's decision to confiscate his property. Now, by the cadence of the words and the nature of the conversation, we have reached a stage where the nobles have recovered from the initial shock and have come to deliberate what is to be done.

It is as deliberate and static as a committee-meeting, with Northumberland in the chair. He is the one link with what has gone before, having had three lines and a half in the preceding scene. When the two scenes were run into one, Ross and Willoughby were brought on with the king, but had been given nothing to do and even less to say than the queen, who at least has one line on her entry and a couplet spoken to her at the end. To all intents and purposes, Ross and Willoughby need not be there at all, and it is much better, dramatically, that they should not be. Standing about with nothing to do or say, and with no indication who they are or why they are there, they give the impression of being nonentities brought in merely to dress the stage. Kept back till now, they assume, and retain, a different function in the drama. We begin to know who they are because, having just met them, we listen to what they say.

The steady pace of the scene gives the audience information. Northumberland tells the lords, and the spectators, certain relevant facts, and as a result, Ross and Willoughby tell him, and the spectators, their feelings, from which we gather the general feelings of England. Then Northumberland gradually reveals the news of Bolingbroke's plans for a landing in the north with 3,000 men, and the lords are resolute to join him. By the end of his narration, the head-shaking despondency of Ross has given way to excitement and eagerness for action. Willoughby echoes him in a rhyming line, and we are left with the feeling that the machinery of support for Bolingbroke, and opposition to Richard, has begun to move.

To this determination, the lightness and poetry of the next scene make an effective contrast. The conversation between the queen and her husband's favourites reveals their apprehension and uncertainty; isolated from the progress of events they pass the time, and try to allay their own and each other's fears, by 'conceits' of self-analysis couched in phrases of real beauty. To the bad news brought by Green they can offer nothing but acceptance and despair, and York, when he comes in to corroborate it, is in little better case. Flustered and uncertain, conscious of his own inadequacy in this crisis and resentful of the king's conduct that has brought it about, he feels that some prompt action ought to be taken, but shows, in a series of false starts, that he has no real notion what should be done first. And in the course of all this, without departing from his depiction of character and situation alike, Shakespeare has put before his audience the dilemma that faces not only the characters but the spectators themselves. Both antagonists, the king to whom the nobles are bound by instincts of loyalty and the subject whom that king has so deeply and unquestionably wronged, have claims upon our sympathy, and it is increasingly difficult to take sides. We see York's position, and can understand his attitude, but at least we are not saddled with the additional burden of his responsibilities. Observing these events and emotions from outside, we are not too badly disturbed to enjoy at the same time the language in which they are brought before us.

Bolingbroke, on his first reappearance, has very little to say. It is Northumberland who does most of the talking, and who seems to have the management of affairs, presenting his son Harry Percy, and the lords Ross and Willoughby, as they come in succession to offer their support. The returned exile is careful and restrained in his demands, and York, when he arrives, is at once indignant, straightforward, flustered and slightly absurd, beginning sternly with a denunciation of Bolingbroke's homage as 'deceivable and false', and then fussily tut-tutting, talking about his nephew's 'banished and forbidden legs'—an array of consonants and short vowels which cannot be made gravely impressive—and falling back on what would have happened if he himself had been all that he was in his younger days. Bolingbroke is still courteous and reasonable, his three friends with only one line each give him cumulative support, and York's protests, though still emphatic, lead up to his considered judgement, which comes as a characteristic anticlimax—'I do remain as neuter'. Having said that, he is anxious to end the interview as soon as possible, and rounds off the scene with a couple of sententious rhymes that form an entirely appropriate close.

From this point onward we are increasingly hampered by our knowledge not so much of history as of this particular play. Where the original spectators had a reasonably good idea, from legends or history-books, of what ultimately happened to Bolingbroke and to Richard, they still had no means of knowing, and all the more interest in seeing and hearing, just *how* it happened, and how the players were going to reproduce it before them. It is hard for us, on the other hand, to keep our minds from going ahead in anticipation of the great scenes that we know are to follow, and leap-frogging over the subtleties of the intermediate scenes and speeches that have done so much to prepare the ground for them. Putting out of our minds, if such a thing be possible, our foreknowledge of well-known and justly-admired episodes like the confrontation at Flint castle, the queen's reception of bad news in the garden at Langley, and the great abdication scene itself, we may find unexpected dramatic force in the very sound of the words in which the story is set before us, and the atmosphere prepared.

This combination of information and atmosphere is very subtly contrived in the succeeding scenes. It takes a Welsh captain only four lines to tell Salisbury—and the audience—that the king's Welsh allies are tired of waiting for him and are going home; the rest of the short scene is a passage of expressive and unexpected beauty. Salisbury's protest is brief and unavailing, and we see Richard's fortunes beginning to fail, even before his homecoming. By contrast, Bolingbroke's condemnation of Bushy and Green has a note of finality from its very opening. A half-line of four

monosyllables is enough to set the tone. There is no need to
waste any time; the matter has been decided, the decision
is final, and the judge is at once pronouncing sentence and
making sure that the prisoners, and the audience, understand
the reason for it. The first charge is their misleading and cor-
ruption of the king; the speaker's own wrongs come afterwards and are described with controlled eloquence that is
the more powerful because of its restraint. There is no
pleading, no speech in mitigation; death is the inevitable
sentence, and the prisoners know it. Like Rivers, Vaughan
and Grey in *Richard III,* they have a line or two each in
acceptance, but here their last words fall into a rhyming
quatrain, as in the old, happier days at Richard's court.
The final instruction is given, 'My lord Northumberland,
see them dispatch'd', and with that last harsh word, final
as the crash of an axe, the court rises, and Bolingbroke
concerns himself with sending messages of reassurance to
the queen. The concluding couplet is broken by a line
indicating what he imagines to be his next task, namely
to deal with the Welsh opposition which we know in advance
to have given up its task and dispersed. After that, he looks
forward to what he describes as 'holiday', the repeal of his
banishment and the peaceful enjoyment of his patrimony.

It is not he, but Northumberland and the rebel lords, who
have in mind the ultimate object of pulling down the king;
not Bolingbroke's arrival, but his abandonment by his own
subjects, that inspires Richard to those flights of poetry
and pathos that have made the part famous. In the two great
scenes of Richard's return from Ireland and his meeting with
Bolingbroke at Flint, Burbage has been given every chance
to display his famous versatility. Richard is Richard still,
but shows us another and a more admirable side of his many-
sided character. Not only are these scenes filled with poetic
imagery; the return to rhyme gives the effect of tremendous,
and successful, effort to control the emotions. His first
rhymed couplet rounds off an expression of extravagant
self-confidence, but the sudden shock of the bad news
brought by Salisbury strikes him dumb and pale, to the
consternation of those about him. When at last he begins to
speak again, his use of a quatrain and couplet suggests a man

almost at the end of his self-control, groping desperately for the most precise, formal way of expressing himself and avoiding the humiliation of a complete breakdown. Something of the sort is to be seen in the way the bringers of bad news convey their tidings in speeches that end with the formality of rhyme or assonance. One turns to deliberately artificial forms when the bare natural expression is too shocking or distressing to be borne. Scrope in his turn seeks refuge in the formality of a quatrain, carefully choosing his words to lengthen out the prelude to the bitter news that must come at last, 'Your uncle York is joined with Bolingbroke'. That is the final blow, and Richard realises that there is no hope left.

After this, Richard—with Burbage as his interpreter—plays up the situation to the very fullest, and the tragedy of Bolingbroke begins. Again and again, in plain straightforward language, he maintains that he comes for no more than the lands and title that he has inherited, but Northumberland is obviously not content with this, while it is Richard himself who continually maintains that Bolingbroke really has his eye on the crown. It is Northumberland, not Bolingbroke, who omits the customary obeisance and has to be reminded of it; Bolingbroke, who punctiliously kneels before his sovereign, gets no thanks but a sarcastic comment on his formality and a hint that he has less honourable intentions. The gardeners' scene that follows is full of poetry, and at the same time makes it clear to the queen and the audience together that it is the increasing, overwhelming mass of the English nobility on Bolingbroke's side that 'weighs King Richard down', and is likely to deprive him of his throne.

But before that happens, there comes another scene in which we see, and hear, Bolingbroke intent on his honourable task of clearing up mysteries and, as far as possible, righting wrongs. Once again he is in the judgement seat, and once again a short half-line command, consonantal and abrupt, brings a man to the bar before him. To our surprise, for so much has happened in between, we are at the question that sparked off the conflict with which the play began, namely who murdered the duke of Gloucester? Who arranged it with the king (whom everyone now admits to have been

behind it) and who actually did the deed? Bagot's reply comes
out slowly and ominously (it is not a line that can be hurried)
and builds up relentlessly to the uttering of a name, and a
name that falls into the expectant silence like a stone into
a pool. 'Then set before my face the lord Aumerle.' We can
almost hear the greater silence that follows, until Bolingbroke
calls upon Aumerle to confront his accuser. Bagot respect-
fully but firmly taxes him with having boasted of the murder,
and includes a reference to other remarks directed against
Bolingbroke himself.

Aumerle's answer is quick, furious and almost hysterical,
culminating with the act of dashing down a gage as a
challenge of battle, and giving his opponent the lie. For a
moment it looks as if we were going to have the first scene
all over again, with Bolingbroke doing for this challenge
what John of Gaunt did for the earlier one, but now there
is a difference. Fitzwater, Percy and an unnamed lord fling
down their gages, and Aumerle finds himself outfaced and
contradicted on every side. Surrey alone contradicts and
challenges Fitzwater, who in reply cites a more damning
accusation of Aumerle, said to have been uttered by the
banished Norfolk. Bolingbroke intervenes at this point,
suspending all further recrimination till his old adversary
can be recalled from banishment, but in grave and sonorous
tones the bishop of Carlisle tells the assembly the news of
Norfolk's death. This comes as a shock to all, and puts an
end to further dispute. Bolingbroke's voice instinctively takes
on the gravity of the bishop's, and Aumerle's case, and the
challenges against him, are deferred until a day can be
appointed for the trial.

This scene has been frequently under-estimated, as being
repetitive and slightly absurd, with the gradual accumulation
of gloves and hoods upon the floor, and the necessity of
clearing them out of the way for the next scene, but this is
possibly due to disregard of the importance of Aumerle.
Hitherto we have seen him as a faithful echo of Richard,
loyal to him and wittily ill-natured in his little conversation
about 'high Hereford' after the latter's banishment. Now we
find him accused of something far more serious, with adversaries rising against him wherever he looks, and in the fury

of his reaction he is revealed as potentially dangerous. The tension of the scene is not relaxed, but suspended, when Bolingbroke puts an end to it for the time being, and the various gages are impounded, under his eye, by the officers of the court. (There is all the difference between doing this in the scene, as a necessary part of the action, and leaving it to be done afterwards by the stage-hands or attendants and causing thereby a slight stage wait and a break in the dramatic tension.) When he has ascended the throne, after Carlisle's protest and arrest by Northumberland, he reminds the quarrelling nobles that they too are under arrest and must arrange about bail, and that he himself stands under no obligation to any of them.

Throughout the scene of Richard's abdication, Bolingbroke is considerate and restrained. It is Northumberland who undertakes the management of affairs, and uses a bullying tone throughout, grumbling when Bolingbroke tries to check him. The latter is so taciturn that Richard rallies him upon his silence and is met with an answer that is so shrewd and apposite that he cannot help admiring it. His own relish of words, as in the line 'Good king, *great* king—and yet not greatly good', is echoed in Bolingbroke's comment over the shattered mirror,

> The shadow of your sorrow hath destroy'd
> The shadow of your face,

which Richard unexpectedly welcomes. Then, when the transfer-ceremony is over, and almost all the participants have left the stage, the regretful lines of the bishop and the abbot are followed by a fierce couplet from Aumerle in which he frankly demands a plot to 'rid the realm' of its newly-appointed king. History is indeed repeating itself; a quarrel, accusation and counter-accusation have led to fierce resentment against authority, this time with still more serious results. Aumerle has been involved in a murder case before; now it appears that he is urging not revolt but assassination.

Meanwhile, Burbage has been given another chance to display his qualities. In *Romeo and Juliet*, as we have seen, the part of the young lover seems likely to have been too

young for him, but that was a matter of dramatic require-
ment, not of technique. Now, in his parting with his queen,
he has a scene of practically operatic quality, rich in beauty
and pathos. First come solo passages for queen and captive
in turn, each purporting to answer the other but developing
into an independent speech, like strophe and antistrophe,
giving the scene a lyrical form at once. Breaking in on this
comes the entry of Northumberland, with four brusque
lines announcing the separate destinies of the lovers, and the
note is momentarily changed. Richard utters a grave, quiet
prophecy of what will happen when matters have gone a
stage further, all the more serious because it is based not
only on Northumberland's actions but on his character, and
Northumberland practically admits as much, with the grim
line 'My guilt be on my head, and there an end'.

The interlude is over, the moment of parting is actually
upon them, and the two exiles take leave of each other in
what is in fact a passionate duet. Here, the use of rhyme
takes the place of music; it is surely for this scene that
Shakespeare has made the queen a woman, not the child of
12 that she really was, and for once we see Richard overcome
with grief and pity for someone other than himself. They are
separated at last, she knows that she will never seen him
again, and we in the audience will see him only once, and
that when he is waiting on the very threshold of death.

But before that moment there occurs an episode which
is too often underrated in reading and neglected in performance. At the beginning and end of the deposition scene we
have come to learn a good deal more about the character
and potentialities of Aumerle; now we are to see their
immediate results culminating in the death of the king
whom he has really loved, and, according to his own
lights, loyally served. In that service he readily disregards
the fact that he has sworn fealty to the king's successor, and
allowed his father to stand surety for him, and that he has
been treated with great clemency, suffering only the loss
of the step in rank. All this comes out in plain, easy language
following York's description of the entry of Richard and
Bolingbroke into London, and this scene, with the young
man's laconic and sulky replies to his father's attempts at

conversation, creates an atmosphere of rather humdrum domestic tranquility that is rudely broken by the discovery of the treasonable document that he carries at his breast.

The effect is, and should be, abrupt and shocking. York has appeared hitherto as Shakespeare's equivalent of Sir Pelham Wodehouse's Lord Emsworth, so brilliantly described, on his first introduction, as 'that amiable and boneheaded peer'. Now, like Lord Emsworth on certain memorable occasions, he is touched to the very depths of his being, and his reactions, though exaggerated to the point of absurdity, reveal an unexpected strength of character. In a matter of personal honour, honesty and conduct he is on his own ground, and with no hesitation whatever he is shouting for his boots, ordering round his horse, and standing no nonsense from his wife or son. The little episode of the servant with the boots gives occasion for a heightening of the tension, with the duchess trying to check the man, Aumerle terrified into inaction, and the old gentleman unexpectedly dominating the scene, pulling on his boots in disregard of his lady's protestations and bucketing off to Windsor to avert the danger by laying the whole matter before the king. The sense of frenzied action is kept up in the lines after his departure, and it is interesting to note that the scene is *not* rounded off with a couplet. Rhyme, here, would produce an instinctive slowing-down of speech and thought at a moment when the keynote is one of urgent haste, and we are left with the feeling that the scene has not been brought to a close, but is being carried on with the utmost rapidity elsewhere. It is a repetition, and an intensification, of an effect made much earlier in the play, when Richard and his entourage set off to visit the dying John of Gaunt, and throws the interest forward to the expected meeting.

Another early effect is repeated here, in reverse. We have seen how the desolation of the widowed duchess of Gloucester is made to give place to the brisk preliminaries for the assault-at-arms. This time, a scene of desperate activity is immediately succeeded by one of complete contrast, both vocal and dramatic. We have been told of conspiracy against the life of the king, we have seen the beginning of a neck-and-neck race to seek the king's justice or the king's pardon, and now we are given our first glimpse of the successful usurper at last established in his power, and both sound and sentiment of the opening line tell us how little he is enjoying it. The slow, dragging syllables of 'Can no man tell me of my unthrifty son?' suggest a weight of weariness, and a kind of helpless distaste for the answer, and sure enough, when it comes it is not encouraging. By the text of the play, as distinct from our own preconceived ideas, Bolingbroke has not come originally to seek the throne; it is the ambition of the Percies that has stirred up the nobles to put him there, and he has already said how little cause he has to thank them.

The latter part of the scene provides an interesting example of Shakespeare's use, in this play, of rhymed and unrhymed verse to express different degrees of tension. Aumerle's entry, and his father's indignant arrival hard upon his heels, are expressed in passionate blank verse, the son's fear and the father's anger being contrasted with Henry's control of the situation and of himself. Not until he has shown his readiness to 'excuse this deadly blot' does the dialogue go into rhyme, and then only with concluding couplets that suggest that the judgement is resentfully accepted, and the episode has come to an unwelcome end.

But in fact matters are very different. In a moment the duchess is at the door, and with her arrival the situation, in the new king's own words, 'is alter'd from a serious thing'. As in the opening scene of the play, the use of rhyme brings the passion under some degree of control. King Henry is able to make himself pleasant and encouraging by taking the situation lightly, even in the very words he chooses when telling Aumerle to unlock the door. He has granted a pardon, and is going to stand by it, though in their passionate protest and counter-protest the duke and duchess hardly give him the chance to say so. They are in the presence of their king, and must address to him, in as formal terms as may be, the adjurations they are aiming at each other. When desperation drives the duchess to address her husband directly, she preserves the proprieties by making her speech even more formal and courtly, couching it in the form of a highly   artificial argument, as if it were done for the amusement of the listening king, upon whom everything depends. She is not to be put off by kindness and courtesy; the word she is waiting for is 'pardon', and she will not rise from her knees until she hears it, and hears it repeated, to make sure that she has heard aright.

Then, at long last, we feel the tension released. Henry abandons the formal couplet and goes back to straight blank verse, making arrangements at once to deal with the other conspirators and incidentally doing the best thing possible for the frustrated and humiliated York by showing him confidence and giving him something to do, and to do at once. There is briskness and efficiency in the rhymes that end the scene, and it may well be queried whether the convention of despising and omitting it has not done something to impair the reputation of the play. The text is not poetry, but it should not be underestimated on that account, because, rightly understood, it is drama, and expository drama at that, since it reveals the danger in which the new king stands, and the risk he must continue to run while the imprisoned Richard remains alive.

A little scene of less than a dozen lines drives this point home and introduces Sir Piers of Exton, telling us at once what he is going to do, and why. Once again this technique intensifies the irony of what follows. As we were given an indication of the spirit in which the king and queen were going to visit the dying Gaunt, so we now see the doom that is rushing upon king Richard in his prison. Like Gaunt, and to a still   greater extent, Richard is given a passage of great poetry and beauty, made the more poignant by ignorance of what is to come. It would give Burbage every chance to show his versatility at its height. Richard the prisoner is trying to discipline himself by analysing his thoughts and persuade himself into a philosopher's acceptance of his position; the sound of music instantly stirs up Richard the artist, and leads him on to the self-contemplation and self-pity that had accompanied his surrender to Bolingbroke, and the arrival of the groom lifts him out of that, to earn our sympathy again by his simple appreciation of the man's kindness. And then, last of all, comes a quality that author and actor have kept to the end. The room suddenly fills with armed men, and Richard shows his physical energy and undaunted spirit. Unarmed himself, he seizes a weapon, kills two of his adversaries and dies fighting. It is a whirlwind finish to a scene that has been designedly static and contemplative throughout.

It is interesting to see how rhyme takes over here, and in the old way, using formality to calm the storm and control the emotion. After that first cry of execration against his death-blow, Richard uses his last reserve of strength to speak with dignity, and to die decorously like a king. It is only natural that Exton should be impressed, and instinctively end in the same key, and this key is maintained, almost unvaried, through the short scene that ends the play. Once more we are at court, in the presence of a king who is receiving official reports and making official acknowledgements and anncouncements. Those reports and announcements are being given in public, and the effect of official language is conveyed by the formality of rhyme. Even at the news of Richard's death, and the production of his body, the new king keeps control of himself; his denunciation of Exton is uncompromising, and all the more terrible because it is so deliberate and comes from the head as well as the heart. Passionate, self-revealing emotion has died, magnificently, in the scene before, and for those who survive there is nothing left but the thankless business of state.

Chapter Eight

KINGS, PRINCES AND THE VOICE OF AUTHORITY

SHAKESPEARE'S NEXT historical play differs so widely from *Richard II* in superficial appearance that we may be freely forgiven for overlooking, at first sight, the very close relation between the two. *King John* has nothing of the regular form of the earlier play; we have always been told that it was a re-hash of an earlier work by someone else, and its general outline approximates more closely to *I Henry VI* in that instead of being a continuous narrative of cause and consequence it is a string of effective episodes out of a history-book, and not such a helpful history-book at that. Edward Hall, who told the story of Richard, was a deliberate historian, careful to indicate the points of character and circumstance that led to the rise and fall of the houses of Lancaster and York, and their ultimate supersession by the Tudors. Holinshed, by contrast, was not so much an author as an editor, covering a far larger field and collecting his material from other writers of varying views and widely-varied quality. Much of his work is a series of acknowledged transcriptions, subjected of course to editorial cuts, glosses and minor amendments but still ascribed, in the margin, to their various authors. Shakespeare's *King John,* and the earlier *Troublesome Raigne of King John,* from which it was adapted, are in their construction as typical of Holinshed as *Richard II* is typical of Hall.

How, then, can we account for Shakespeare's return to a form which he himself had done much to supersede? It may not be far-fetched to suggest that Burbage himself provides the answer. The theatre-boy of the old pre-Shakespearean days had grown up in the atmosphere of those early dramas and would have had every chance of knowing, seeing, and

admiring the old *Troublesome Raigne,* and particularly one
part of it that would appeal to a boy's fancy. The shrewd,
heroic, breezy Bastard of Faulconbridge is a person that
many a boy would want to emulate, and a character that
many a theatre-boy would long to play when he grew up.
And, moreover, now, if ever, was the time to play it.
Richard II had been a success, it was important to follow
it up with another success before the first grew stale, and
here was a part as different from Richard as possible, and
at the same time quite as effective in the right hands. An
actor with a definite, impressive personality has a difficult
task before him if he is to be at once an artistic and a commercial success. People come to the theatre to see him with
a preconceived notion of what they want, and what they
expect, and they must not be entirely disappointed. On
the other hand, they will want something fresh as well,
whether or not they consciously realise it, and they will
not long be content with repetitions of 'the mixture as
before'. The favourite must be familiar and original at the
same time, and it needs a good actor and a good playwright
to produce such a result between them.

But that combination was just what the Chamberlain's
men had got. The old two-part play was in print, and with
it before him Shakespeare was able to take over characters,
incidents, sentiments, odd turns of phrase and what there
was in the way of a plot, and make from them a new version
cut to the measure of the company he served. Like *Richard II*
it has three or four effective parts for boy-actresses, all of
them rather better than Richard's queen or the duchesses
of Gloucester and York, and nothing for the clowns. Possibly
Kempe, the Peter of *Romeo and Juliet,* was resting, or doing
a dance-and-broad-comedy act elsewhere, but it is noticeable
that both these plays do their work without the usual intervention of cheerful and colloquial prose. Light relief there is,
but in this play it is the Burbage part that has to provide it
On the other hand, there is a new feature in the introduction
of a highly emotional part for a small boy. Probably a *very*
small boy, since he has to die on the stage and his dead body
has to be picked up, without effort, by a single actor, while
another stands by and comments on the ease with which he

does it. Possibly the part was played by the Hermia-Katherina-Luciana performer, possibly by someone smaller still, who was about the theatre, if not officially on the strength of the company, and was learning the profession even as Burbage had learnt it before him.

Like *Richard II,* this play also opens with a piece of expressive sound. The peremptory quality of its first line reminds one of the other play's Northumberland—it may very well have been written for the same actor—and with no delay whatever it shows the spectators what the situation is. Nothing essential has gone before; the very opening of the play is the opening of a state occasion, with a king giving audience to an ambassador of France. The latter is roundly asked to give his message, his answer tells us all we need to know at the moment, and we go on from there. It is an admirable beginning, and Shakespeare used it again, many years later, to open the third act of *Cymbeline,* where the same situation occurs, though this time the omission of the ambassador's name makes Cymbeline's 'Now say, what would Augustus Caesar with us?' appreciably less abrupt than the 'Now say, Chatillon, what would France with us?' of the present play.

There is less rhyme throughout than there was in *Richard II,* but then there is less occasion for Court politeness and restraint, though Queen Elinor has a discreet couplet to round off an accurate but indiscreet comment on John's rights in France. The situation calls for it, however, when the question of the Faulconbridge inheritance comes under discussion. What might be a painful and embarrassing subject is lightened by the Bastard's consistent refusal to treat it over-seriously. His couplets about the family likeness of the Faulconbridges have a cheerful flippancy that precludes any suggestion of bitterness and 'sour grapes', and when he has renounced his patrimony and entered the service of his newly-acknowledged grandmother he talks in couplet and quatrain with the lightness of a 13th-century Berowne so long as he is in company. Left alone, he is still flippant, though in ordinary unrhymed verse, but at the end of the act he heartens his mother with couplet and quatrain once more, bringing in a compliment to her attractiveness as he bears her off to display her to his real father's family.

Lady Faulconbridge does not appear again, but this play gives more opportunity than *Richard II* to the boy-actresses in general. In the earlier play, the queen's part consisted of solo work, except in her last great duet with the king; here the unbroken voices are given a chance to sound in relation to each other. Queen Elinor has shown her mettle in the first half-dozen lines of the play, and she is matched with a worthy antagonist in her exchanges with Constance under the walls of Angers. In the latter part of this scene, Blanche of Spain is introduced, with very little to say as yet but with considerable significance to the plans and passions of the opposing kings. In her next scene she has a chance of standing out; her voice is heard pleading while Constance is alternating between rage and lamentation and cursing the wedding-day in language echoing Job's curse upon the day he was born. The blustering of Austria, the sonority of Pandulph, and the vacillations of Philip of France are all blending and contrasting in an almost-operatic ensemble until Philip abandons the alliance under the irresistible pressure of Rome. And, throughout both these scenes, we are conscious of the presence and comments of Arthur of Brittany, not the ambitious youth of 16 or 17 that he in fact was, but a pathetic child, bandied about between his mother and grandmother until he is taken in battle and summarily handed over to be consoled by old Queen Elinor while John drops hints to Hubert, rather as the newly-crowned Richard III has done to Buckingham and Tyrell in the earlier play, about the possibility of his death.

Gradually the women's and boys' voices fade away. Queen Elinor does not appear again after this scene, Blanche has already gone, and Constance has one last display of passionate grief and objurgation before she too passes into oblivion. Only Arthur is left, and with his death we are momentarily in a world of men, until at the end we are given a glimpse of the young prince Henry, probably the performer of Blanche or Elinor in another guise.

Meanwhile, Burbage has had a chance to develop his part by degrees. He has repudiated romance and declared his allegiance to worldly advantage as roundly as Petruchio—or Shaw's Dick Dudgeon, for the matter of that—and his disrespectful remarks to Austria may be taken at first as a natural reaction to knightly solemnity in general and Austria's pomposity in particular, but there is a deeper significance behind, and one that Elizabethan audiences might have been readier to grasp. His jeers at the other's lion-skin mantle are more than rude personal remarks; when he invokes St. George it is ostensibly in his capacity as an alehouse-sign, when he threatens Austria it is not with death but with cuckoldry and ridicule, the 'horned monster' being a familiar emblem for a husband whose wife has been unfaithful to him, but there is a personal feeling underlying it all, however much care he takes to hide it. Lewis the Dauphin, at the beginning of the scene, tells young Arthur that the duke of Austria was responsible for the death of Richard Coeur-de-Lion, audiences in general believed as much, and took it that he wore the lion-skin in token of his triumph, and in the scene immediately before this one they had seen the Bastard universally accepted as Coeur-de-Lion's son. It is natural that he should resent the sight of the great Richard's emblem on the shoulders of his killer, and just as natural—for him—that he should go to all possible lengths to avoid any suggestion of personal feeling or filial piety. All the same, the audiences of Shakespeare's day would expect some manifestation of the relationship, and, sure enough, the author gives them what they expect, but not in the way they have been expecting it. There is no terrific combat, no 'This for my father's death!' in the orthodox melodramatic fashion. There are sounds of battle, the Bastard comes in complaining of the heat of the day, and we realise with a shock that what he is carrying is the severed head of Austria. In the most matter-of-fact way imaginable, the son of Richard Coeur-de-Lion has avenged his father.

Next moment John enters in alarm with the news that his mother has been 'assailed in her tent and ta'en, I fear', only to be met with the easy reassurance

> My lord, I rescued her;
> Her highness is in safety; fear you not.

The Bastard is, when he chooses, an expert in the fine art of understatement, but after this he is never flippant again. One by one John's helpers fall away. Queen Elinor dies, the barons turn from him on the report of Arthur's death, Hubert himself is suspect, and there is no satisfaction to be gained from Pandulph and the Pope. Only the Bastard stays true to him through all, developing and instilling fresh courage at every piece of bad news and prepared to follow his dying master into the dark as readily as Kent at the end of a more tremendous tragedy. But before that, there is work to be done, and the one man who has never been shaken in his courage or his loyalty heads the nobles in homage to the new child-king, and then rallies them with words of reassurance and encouragement to stand fast, in the knowledge that by so doing they may save England yet.

With these two historical plays, and the comedy of *The Merchant of Venice,* that dates from the same period, we get an indication of the main composition of the company and what may be called its vocal orchestration. The three principals would seem to have been Burbage, in his late twenties, and by training, instinct and experience an actor to his fingertips; a graver, possibly older man to carry the 'heavy' parts of Bolingbroke, Hubert and Antonio, and another whose line was a combination of dignity and malevolence, and whom audiences would consequently welcome as Northumberland in *Richard II,* and subsequently as Worcester (a part not often given its full importance), Shylock, and King John. And, of course, the company had enjoyed another important advantage in the return of the Clown. Wherever Kempe may have been since he played Peter in *Romeo and Juliet,* he was back among his old companions now, and Shakespeare could once again write plays with clowns in them, preferably fat clowns; first that 'huge feeder', Launcelot Gobbo, and then—gloriously fattest of fat parts—Falstaff.

Here, for the first time, we find the clown's part closely involved with that of the leading player. Audiences had seen the courtier Berowne, genially satirical, the passionate young nobleman Mercutio, 'sudden and quick in quarrel' and rushing unexpectedly on his death, the spoilt young poet-king Richard, unreliable and yet able to die fighting like a hero, and his cheerful antithesis, the blunt, ever-faithful Faulconbridge, proclaiming allegiance to personal profit in principle and completely disregarding it in practice. Most recently of all had come that too often underrated gallant, the 'scholar and soldier' Bassanio. It is the story of his courtship that runs through *The Merchant of Venice* from the indiscreet borrowing of money from the wrong person at the beginning to the test of the caskets, where he wins his lady by thinking not what he may get with her, but what he is prepared to give for her, and on, beyond the frustrations of the trial scene, to the spisode of the ring, with its revelations, reconciliation and badinage in a moonlit garden. What kind of young hero were the players and play-wright going to put before them next?

A line of Bolingbroke's, already quoted, may well be held to provide the answer. The audience at Burbage's theatre was principally a local audience; its patrons came from a quarter devoted to what Stow calls 'fair houses of merchants' in the neighbourhood of London Wall, and among those merchants, with families to govern, businesses to administer and responsibilities to maintain, there must have been many a one who had had occasion to say, with the new-crowned king Henry, 'Can no man tell me of my unthrifty son?' In a business community, where a successful man would have control of sons and apprentices who ran the risk of getting into bad company and undoing the work of a laborious lifetime, there would be an audience trained and ready to appreciate a reminder that their occupational anxieties might affect even kings, while their wives would have a certain sympathy with a personable young man in danger of being led astray.

We meet the young prince and his tempter in a scene of lively, unrefined conversational prose, and from the very outset we are in great danger of missing its true significance because we know, or think we know, too much about Falstaff already, from the other plays about him, and from having read the later scenes of this one, not to mention critical assessments of him by distinguished Shakespearean scholars. One almost unavoidably comes to this first scene of his with some preconceived notion of Falstaff with philosopher, Falstaff, the fat amorist of Eastcheap, or the Windsor laundry-basket, Falstaff, the unjustifiably lovable old rogue. Looked at, however, as those early audiences had to look at him, he is a different character. In his first half-a-dozen speeches he has admitted himself to be a thief and an associate of thieves, and at first we have every reason to fear that Hal is not much better, so ready is he to identify himself with 'us that are the moon's men', as the slang of the time calls them. It has been a commonplace through the centuries that many a gang of thieves and counterfeiters contains at least one man whose birth, breeding and education have qualified him for a more honourable career, but who has drifted into bad company partly through indolence, partly through curiosity and the desire for excitement and self-glorification. It was a course into which the Elizabethan youth was very likely to be misguided. Parents and employers knew all about it, and would see at once the king's anxiety about his son and Falstaff's keen eye for the advantages of being on intimate terms with the heir-apparent to the throne. His very accusations of Hal's evil influence upon him are an ingenious kind of flattery, as if the young man were already an outstandingly bad character and proud of it, and at Hal's 'Where shall we take a purse to-morrow, Jack?' we fear for a moment that he may be right.

Reassurance comes when Poins enters with news of a chance of profitable robbery at Gad's Hill, and Hal is invited to be one of the party. His reaction is one of real shock and indignant refusal, with none of his former easy banter. It wavers, however, under Falstaff's contemptuous charge of poor-spiritedness, and that ancient argument, 'Oh, come on—be a sport!' that is so hard to resist. For a moment, in fact, he surrenders, and agrees to join in the robbery, just for once, but even in that moment he knows he has made the wrong decision, and he instantly goes back on it, 'come what will', even though it may mean the loss of Falstaff's friendship and his own good name among his tavern companions. When they are gone, it is only with hesitation and reluctance that he agrees to take part in the practical joke suggested by Poins, and only when this last companion has gone does he turn from prose to blank verse—the first passage of verse that we have heard him speak. For the first time we see him alone with his thoughts, and as the sound of the speech changes, so his mood changes with it, and our own with him.

Hindsight, unfortunately, has done much to nullify the importance of this scene. Scholars, audiences, producers and actors have all had the image of the Henry of Agincourt too readily in their minds to see that this is a younger, more vulnerable Henry, and to appreciate the greatness of his temptation and the significance of his ultimate decision. The important point, so frequently overlooked, is that it has not been an easy one. He has had to choose between unenterprising right and exciting, fascinating wrong, and to admit to himself what sort of a life he is leading, and what its end must necessarily be. Here, even before the confrontation with his father in jest in the tavern or in earnest in the council-chamber comes the knowledge that one day the break must come, and he must separate himself from those tavern-companions who are the only friends he knows. If he has not yet touched pitch, his fingers have lightly brushed an undeniably sticky surface, and he knows how near he has come to being defiled. It is a mistake—with all due respect to the many great scholars who have made it—to treat the speech that follows as a cold-blooded explanation of policy. It is drama, and very moving drama at that, and the change from prose to verse brings it more keenly home. Shakespeare is doing here what he does in certain passages elsewhere, notably the conversation between Brutus and Cassius at the beginning of *Julius Caesar*. A character is telling the audience something it needs to know, and at the same time revealing something of his own character in the telling.

Let us first consider what the play is about. Its main theme, in both parts of it, is the relation between a father and his son, and the necessarily slow process of the son's 'finding himself' and developing his own character. This is not a thing that can happen all at once, but it is important to show clearly at the outset that it can happen at all, and to prevent spectators from falling into the error of the citizen's wife in *The Knight of the Burning Pestle*, who persists in decrying Jasper, the hero of the play she is watching, and extending all her sympathy to the idiotic Humphrey. In *Richard III*, Burbage had lost no time in explaining that he was going to be a villain; in this play he must make it clear, as early as possible, that he is not.

All the same, Hal will not find it easy to live up to his good intentions, and he knows it. Like St. Augustine with his famous prayer, 'Give me chastity and continence, but please, not just yet', he would rather not make a clean, abrupt break with his daily life and nightly companions. It is not a heroic attitude, but it is a very human one, and he is doing his best to persuade himself that it is justifiable, and that if he spends a little more time in his dubious courses his ultimate reputation will be all the better for it. So it will, but as yet he does not know, and the spectators have not been shown, how great a price he will have to pay for it when the break comes, on his coronation-day, and when, later still, he has to let the bottle-nosed Bardolph go to the gallows for breach of his own strict instructions about honesty and discipline.

In the very next speech, at the opening of the next scene, we see his father doing just the same thing, and announcing that hitherto he has been too easy-going, but now he 'will from henceforth rather be himself'. This precipitates a breach with the great house of the Percies, who had been instrumental in raising him to the throne, and once again the choice of words brings out the variety of the voices and the varying pace of their utterance. Northumberland is gravely discreet and non-committal, as befits the practical trimmer that he was; Hotspur by contrast breaks out into a whirlwind of words, so that what was meant for an explanation develops into a passionate and indignant protest, which Sir Walter Blunt does his best to modify by the ponderous, legalistic pronouncement of his considered opinion, and the sound of the king's words and the succession of his arguments reveal that he is rapidly losing his temper. So, in his turn, is Hotspur, and when the king has stormed away with a final threat, the field is clear for the return of the quiet, keen-eyed Worcester, who has kept his head and his temper and, sharing neither the rage of Hotspur nor the apprehensions of Northumberland, is infinitely more dangerous than either of them. Most ominous of all, he is in no hurry, but can afford to wait until Hotspur's passion has practically blown itself out. He knows his nephew's character through and through, and in two lines he sums up the qualities that made Hotspur such a pleasure to listen to and such a nuisance as a fellow-conspirator.

> He apprehends a world of figures here,
> But not the form of what he should attend.

It would be diffult to improve on that as a summary of Hotspur's character and, at the same time, a revelation of Worcester's own.

Now follows a scene of prose—and what prose! We have come beyond the ridicule of peasants and fantastics, the brief backchat of servants in the great houses of Italy, or of 'rude mechanicals' in Athens, past even the interchange of personalities and arguments between the prince and the company he keeps. Here the listeners are confronted with life as it goes on in London and its outskirts, in the world of road transport and those who handle it and cater for its activities in the early morning, when most respectable citizens are still in bed. The carriers with their two-o'clock-in-the-morning start, calling repeatedly for the ostler and commenting on the shortcomings of the inn; Gadshill, the 'setter' or go-between, making arrangements with the corrupt inn-chamberlain on the backstairs (it was a common belief that inn-chamberlains had a regular understanding with the local thieves) and trying meanwhile both to steal the carriers' lantern and to get information about their own journey, and the chamberlain himself, in alliance with Gadshill, and at the same time under no illusions about him, combine to give the atmosphere of a dark, chilly morning and, incidentally, of the sort of life and company to which the prince was so nearly committing himself. They are all small parts, and yet all rewarding, because the author has been so generous with his good lines and expressive strokes of character. Gadshill, who has very little to do, might be reckoned a thankless little part were it not redeemed by his expressive comments on his fellows and scorn of 'mad mustachio purple-hued malt-worms', and the chamberlain comes to life with his professional patronising of Gadshill himself, very much to the latter's annoyance.

When the interest shifts from practical joking to serious conspiracy and rebellion, we are shown again what Shakespeare was beginning to do with prose, in Hotspur's soliloquy over a letter from an unnamed correspondent whom he has rather injudiciously invited to join him in the rising. Thoughts and words come tumbling out in a swift, passionate spate, that denotes the very absence of coherence and self-control and is the absolute antithesis to the steadying rhymed couplets that we have seen denoting passions kept, with difficulty, in hand. Hotspur has been incoherent in verse after his quarrel with the king in council; now that he is alone he has gone a stage further and abandoned all attempt to marshal his arguments. Every sentence he reads in the letter starts him off on a fresh line of indignation, chiefly because he has made a bad mistake and knows it. He admits that he could 'divide himself and go to buffets' for inviting a man who is not, after all, prepared to believe in the enterprise, and who will in all probability do something to check it if it is not set on foot at once, ready or no. It is only with the decision to start the rebellion that the emotions of the scene are brought down, with Lady Percy as intermediary, to the regularity of verse. His badinage with someone whom he can tease and patronise puts him into good humour with himself again, and he goes eagerly on to the task that by his own lack of judgement he has prematurely set in motion.

Back at the tavern we are given more prose in still greater variety; first the scene between Hal, Poins and Francis the pot-boy, which seems rather poor fun on the printed page but comes to life on the lips of experienced comedians, like the 'patter' of popular present-day stars of music-hall or television. Burbage, as the prince, has the chance to let himself go with another string of bewildering and uncomplimentary epithets that come trippingly off the tongue and end in absurdity foreshadowing the clown in *Twelfth Night* who had discoursed of Pigrogromitus and the Vapians, and come to the conclusion that the Myrmidons were no bottle-alehouses.

From this whirlwind of nonsense we come back to Falstaff and his development into the Falstaff we know. There have been hints of it in his conversation at the time of the robbery, but now he is at the height of his performance as a gentleman of the old school, deploring the decadence of the present generation, but still standing fast as an upholder of standards now regrettably ignored. It is outrageous, impressive and exceedingly funny. Contradicted and outfaced at all points, from the matter of drink to that of personal cowardice, he is irrepressible and defiant, and comes up smiling, reaching his climax at that genial roar of 'By the Lord, I knew ye as well as he that made ye', and his explanation of the importance of 'instinct' as a guiding influence on his behaviour. This scene, perhaps, does more than any other to establish him in our minds as a delightful though disreputable character, and tempt us to forget him as a bad influence on the prince. The only person who shows any consciousness of this latter aspect is the prince himself, and when it is his turn to impersonate his father he passes gradually from another string of epithets (how Shakespeare must have enjoyed writing them and Burbage delivering them!) to a serious four-word warning of what will have to be done some day. It comes as something quite unexpected by the hearers, Falstaff himself is momentarily at a loss, and the prince has a chance to put his resolution into practice, if he can bring himself to do it. No one knows— even Hal, we may imagine, is not quite sure—what is going to happen next, and whether the jest is going to turn to unwelcome earnest, but we know that a possible chance of breaking loose from the temptations of bad company has come at last, and may never come so favourably again. And, while we all wait for the next word, there comes a sudden interruption from outside, an interruption that is to be used again in a more famous play, and that is still to be heard, carrying alarm and apprehension with it, in certain quarters to-day. Someone, obviously someone in authority, is beating on the door. We can imagine the nature of that knocking from the manner of its reception, for there is more than one guilty conscience in that tavern. Bardolph announces in alarm that 'the sheriff with a most monstrous

watch is at the door', and the Hostess follows him with something more ominous, 'They are come to search the house'.

That means the gallows for highway robbers, if they can
be found there and identified. The separation may be coming
in an entirely unexpected way, and everybody knows it.
Strangest of all, Falstaff, that natural coward, without
instinct, is prepared to face the inevitable—if it really *is*
inevitable—and not disgrace his upbringing when he has to
make his farewell appearance in the hangman's cart. And,
by the same token, this is not the moment for the prince to
desert his disreputable associates. Falstaff is bundled behind
the wall-hangings, the others take refuge upstairs, and Hal
treats the sheriff with courtesy and consideration, but in a
way that rules out any detailed investigation of the premises.
The moment for decision is past; whatever his intentions
may have been a few minutes ago, that thundering on the
door has brought him down on Falstaff's side of the fence,
to use his position and personal charm in opposition to
the forces of law, order and his father's government, and
we cannot blame him. In blandly deceiving, or at least over-
riding, the Sheriff he is technically doing the wrong thing,
but audiences will feel with relief that he has done it for
the right reason.

There is a great deal of hidden craftsmanship in the
construction of the subsequent scene between king Henry
and his son. It starts on a note of grave reproof, as was to
be expected, and as Falstaff himself had foreshadowed in
his own not unskilful imitation, 'Shall the blessed sun of
heaven prove a micher and eat blackberries? A question
not to be asked'. The king has not the Euphuistic antithesis
and clause-balancing of Falstaff, but the general argument is
the same, and the prince is prepared for it, coming out
with a respectful disclaimer, but he is obviously unprepared
for what comes next—a frank statement of what other
people think of him and what he has already lost in position,
prospects and general reputation. He has no defence against
this, and can only promise to be 'more himself'—an unconscious echo of his father's words to the Percies in the
council-chamber, when he put forward the same promise
as a threat. Indeed, we can see, though the prince cannot, a

certain irony in Henry's description of his own technique of exclusiveness and withdrawal. It does not quite tally with what the deposed Richard said in the earlier play, about his policy of courting the commons and dutifully unbonneting to oyster-wenches, and his expressed admiration of Hotspur as the victor of Holmedon has little to do with the things he said to him and about him when he thought the Crown was not getting its fair share of the booty. In a good many of his parent-and-child confrontations Shakespeare makes the parent start with a justified complaint and become testy and unreasonable in the course of the argument. It is liable to happen in real life, and we can be sure that many young men in Shakespeare's audience knew it, and had experienced it in their relations with their fathers or their employers.

This tendency may not be particularly commendable in principle, but it is often effective in practice, and it is so here. The prince breaks out in passionate protest and repentance, and for the first time we see something of his affection for his father and the value he sets on that father's good opinion. The extravagance of his language, so different from the easy-going banter of his conversation among his ordinary companions, is yet typical of the passionate sincerity of his good intentions, and shows the same basic line of thought as his earlier soliloquy. As with his former indiscretions, so with his loss of reputation, and his admitted inferiority to Hotspur; he cannot deny them, but determines after all to turn them to what advantage he can by treating them as standards to surpass. The lines beginning 'Percy is but my factor, good my lord' are mere boasting and bombast if they are delivered with cheerful self-satisfaction and assurance, but spoken in the key of what has gone before, they are matters of earnest intention, not self-evident fact. The emotional effect of this scene is undeniable; it was something that Burbage could obviously do well, and he had done it before with great success. No doubt Shakespeare trusted that audiences would not notice the resemblance, but this passionate pleading and promises of amendment are just in the manner of Richard of Glouces-ter's successful wooing of Lady Anne. The reassurance is effective; the king turns at once from contemplation to his old Bolingbroke efficiency, greets Sir Walter Blunt's news of the rebels' assembly with an outline of the action that is already being taken to deal with it, and at once finds a place in that action for his reconciled son. The choice of words and the brisk pace of the lines are expressive evidence that the king's private anxiety is over for the moment, and he can turn unreservedly to the matter in hand.

What has been begun in words is confirmed in action on the battlefield. Burbage is allowed to display his ability as a swordsman in two fights of different character. The first comes with a ringing entry-line 'Hold up thy head, vile Scot', when he arrives in the nick of time to rescue his father from the sword of Douglas, and the Scot is driven out while the king recovers his breath and goes off at once to answer an appeal for help elsewhere. The second follows hard upon it, but is prefaced by a few lines of dialogue and, almost certainly, by a moment of dramatic and expressive silence (there is not time for many of these in Shakespeare, but here it may be claimed for one of them) when in this final scene of the play Hal and Hotspur at last stand face to face. Each has heard much, and said a good deal, about the other, but this is their first confrontation, and they both know that it is likely to be their last. Hotspur, in fact, frankly and expressively says so, and unwisely utters a word of regret that the prince is not likely to give him a better fight. He has made the mistake of underrating his opponent, his quick, petulant line, 'I can no longer brook thy vanities' shows that he is once more losing his patience and his temper, and he rushes to the attack without more ado. Both combatants regard the fight as a sporting event of the first magnitude, quite apart from its being a matter of life and death, and one which may affect the success of the rebellion and the very destiny of England. As a defeated jouster in the lists would forfeit his horse and armour to his opponent, and as a present-day boy playing 'conkers' loses his accumulated store, so, in the minds of both combatants, runs the idea that the victor becomes the richer by the military reputation of the vanquished. Hal has spoken of it to his father, and repeated it in answer to Hotspur's slight upon his prowess, and it is in Hotspur's mind as he lies dying on the field.

By the same token it has instantly vanished from Hal's. All he feels is admiration for his adversary and involuntary pity for his end. There is neither boasting nor moralising about the line 'Ill-weav'd ambition, how much art thou shrunk!' To the poet who wrote for that theatre, the players who rehearsed and acted there and the public who went there for their entertainment, a familiar sight on the way was the array of long frames in the tenter-grounds outside the city where new-made cloth was stretched when fresh from the fulling process, and a fine piece of fabric might be spoiled at this last stage by undue shrinkage if the original weaving had not been properly done. Hal's homely north-London-tradesman's metaphor is one of regret for a good thing spoiled because there has been a defect in it somewhere, and in the next moment he is almost apologetically using part of his own trappings to cover the face of the dead. Turning from the man whom he can respect but has never had the chance to know, he finds the supposed corpse of his absolute antithesis—Falstaff, whom he knows too well and cannot honestly respect, but whom, in death at least, he cannot help rather liking. But his work calls him, the battle is not yet over, and he leaves nobility and obesity lying side by side in the unexpected fellowship of death.

It is in the latter part of this play that we begin to notice a new feature that becomes increasingly significant in Shakespeare's verse and, later on, in that of his fellow-playwrights. The practice of now and then ending a line with a dissyllable is not unknown in the earlier plays, but here, in a short scene between the archbishop of York and an otherwise unknown Sir Michael, its repeated use gives a particular form to the speech, and the scene, containing it. It is a scene of brief but helpful exposition, telling the audience of Northumberland's failure through illness, and Glendower's through superstition, and showing the unwisdom of Hotspur's insistence on an immediate battle without the necessary reinforcements. These double endings have an effect of slowing down the pace and allowing a word or a sentence to sink into the mind of the hearer, instead of floating by unheeded on a stream of regular and beautiful sound.

Where rhyme has been used to smooth and modify the utterance of an awkward statement, this form of ending serves to emphasise it and hammer it home, with a sort of authority and quiet certainty achieved by the slowing of the pace and deliberate absence of passion. In the next play it appears more and more frequently; king Henry himself uses it expressively in his midnight conference with his nobles and his opening orders to the page, instinctively abandoning it for his private reflections on sleep. When Lancaster and Westmorland meet the rebel leaders, it is used occasionally by both sides, and has—or, rightly handled, should have—the effect of what in musical terms would be called phrasing. Both sides, at first, speak their feelings eloquently enough, but there comes a time when the archbishop has to put his case not personally, but professionally, as an utterance by a Primate of England from his archiepiscopal throne, and his words become words that cannot be spoken with the even pace of those that have gone before.

> Hear me more plainly.
> I have in equal balance justly weigh'd
> What wrongs our arms may do, what wrongs we suffer,
> And find our griefs heavier than our offences.

That is not an explanation, but a pronouncement, and contrasts with Mowbray's passionate and personal complaint about his father's treatment at the hands of Richard II. When this is courteously but firmly put aside as irrelevant, it is he whose brief interjections have dissyllabic endings, and serve to mark his mood as not in tune—indeed, it never has been; there is too much of Hotspur in him—with that of his allies, and he remains in a bad temper for the rest of the scene.

Herein, also, lies an explanation for the conduct of Lancaster and Westmorland, which at first sight seems very hard to excuse, though Lancaster's opening speech in the interview gives a clear indication of it. It is *because* of the archbishop's dignity and authority, and the confidence he commands and inspires in those who hear him, that he of all people should know better than to use that authority to rise in public opposition to the king and laws of England. The more impressive he has been, the clearer does it become that in his position he could, and should, have sought other ways of laying the national grievances before the king, and cannot be permitted to go scot-free after leading so many others astray. Sir John Colevile, when taxed with being 'a famous rebel' says bluntly

> I am, my lord, but as my betters are
> That led me hither

and is sent to execution with the rest; he has been drawn into treason and by his position and authority has drawn others into it, and he must go.

In *Henry VI,* Shakespeare has shown the tragedy of Englishmen led unwittingly to kill their own kinsfolk by obediently following their overlords into civil wars that they did not understand, and as it had been in the Middle Ages, so it was in the days of Elizabeth, who was to send even her favourite Essex to the scaffold, for the same reason, before this play was old. The arrest and execution of the leaders is, for the king, the greatest relief and happiest news that he could hope for, and that relief and happiness are expressed in the smooth tranquility of the lines in which he greets it.

> O Westmorland, thou art a summer bird
> Which ever in the haunch of winter sings
> The lifting up of day!

It is after the king's death that those dissyllabic endings recur in such numbers and with such effect. The news is given by Warwick to the Lord Chief Justice—and to the audience—in the slow, measured tones of a man who knows he must choose his words carefully. The Chief Justice and, in their turn, the bereaved princes do the same by their very silence, 'like men that had forgot to speak', and the double endings come really into their own in the exchanges between the Justice and the new king. They seem, by their weight and by the way they slow down the diction, to take out the personalities and present a balanced, incontrovertible state-ment of facts. Each in his turn speaks as from the judgement-seat. Henry's stern rebuke

> How might a prince of my great hopes forget
> The great indignities you laid upon me?
> What! rate, rebuke and rashly send to prison
> The immediate heir of England! Was this easy?
> May this be washed in Lethe, and forgotten?

is all the more intense by the fact that it bears out what the late king had said to him, and what he himself had privately admitted, about the results of keeping bad company. The answer, when it comes, is what he knows already and must formally accept and uphold.

> I then did use the person of your father;
> The image of his power lay then in me:
> And, in the administration of his law,
> Whiles I was busy for the commonwealth
> Your highness pleased to forget my place,
> The majesty and power of law and justice,
> The image of the king whom I presented,
> And struck me in my very seat of judgement;
> Whereon, as an offender to your father
> I gave bold way to my authority
> And did commit you.

The argument is unflinching and unanswerable, and the new king unquestioningly accepts it.

The news of one Henry's death and another's succession is brought down to Gloucester by Pistol with such flamboyance as to be incomprehensible at first to the company that sits eating, drinking and singing under the apple-trees As soon as it has sunk in, Falstaff becomes active and practical at once in prose that harks back to his first appearance, and shows him as the unscrupulous old opportunist that he is, ready to make free with other people's horses and hurry up to Westminster in the assurance that he and his friends will have everything their own way. It is an instant, brutal realisation of the late king's prophecy on his deathbed, and will call for instant, uncompromising action if that prophecy is not to be fulfilled. There is a brief scene of noisy, unrefined prose in which we learn one or two more things about Doll Tearsheet and her thieves' kitchen, and at last the inevitable confrontation comes. The new king does his best to avoid a scene, by ordering the Lord Chief Justice to deal with the matter, but Falstaff will not be put off with the king's officers. He continues to hail the king himself, with persistence and familiarity, and draws down on himself that direct, public repudiation that his former friend and pupil would have spared him if he could. The measured, balanced lines come out with implacable sternness; at one dangerous moment there is an allusion to Falstaff's bulk which might be turned into a laugh if he were not quick enough to forbid any such 'fool-born jest' before Falstaff can utter it, but he recovers in time and turns it to advantage with an admission and a warning, 'Presume not that I am the thing I was', and ends with a promise not of punishment but of a pension, and the stately dissyllabic endings come again to hammer it home.

> Some competence of life I will allow you
> That lack of means enforce you not to evil:
> And, as we hear you do reform yourselves,
> We will, according to your strengths and qualities
> Give you advancement.

Each time, the light syllable at the end comes like an echo to emphasise, however slightly, the one that has gone before. Substitute another word, let the Chief Justice say

> Your highness pleased to forget my place,
> The majesty of justice and the law,
> The image of the king for whom I stood
> And struck me in my very judgement-seat

and the passage remains a statement of fact indeed, but has no longer the sternness and gravity of an indictment. It is the same elsewhere; in this play, as we have seen, and in the very different chronicle that follows it. Royal Hal the prince has become Henry the king, and with the exception of a few minutes on the eve of Agincourt, we never see him alone again. His utterances are public pronouncements, his very wooing has a diplomatic object as well as a personal one, and those double-endings, with their consequent slowing-down of the speech to emphasise the meaning, become more and more frequent, whether he is answering an ambassador or condemning a false friend to death for treason. Prince Henry has been developing in character in the course of these three plays, and so, very plainly, has the actor who has played the part in all of them. There is to be no more of the 'romantic juvenile' for him; Burbage is a man of thirty or more by this time, and must have more mature characters to play. The playwright who understands him so well has been developing his own style likewise, and can give the player what he needs. The time is arriving for Hector—and for Hamlet.

Chapter Nine

CONVERSATION AND CONTEMPLATION

BY THE END of the 16th century the players had had to move, as has been mentioned, to a new situation on the South Bank. The Finsbury ventures were abandoned entirely, and the company and their playwright had to attract and retain a new audience of rather a different type, since while the actual crossing of the river was a matter of quick passage and simple boat-hire, the average patron of the old Theatre or Curtain was not very likely to go on foot, with or without his family, the whole way across London to the river bank and the stairs where the wherries lay in readiness. A present-day resident of Hampstead or Finsbury would think twice before going to the Old Vic or the Festival Hall if the railways or omnibuses were on strike, and the comfortable London citizen of 1600 or so would find such an expedition very different from the former pleasant walk to the play-house over Finsbury Fields. The Chamberlain's men could not hope for the continued support of their old patrons; in moving to the South Bank they had to enter into competition with Henslowe's theatres, which were there already, but they had also an additional theatre of a different kind. Years before, James Burbage had acquired, and had fitted up as a regular indoor playhouse, the old hall in the dissolved monastery of Blackfriars, where the choirs of St. Paul's and the Chapels Royal had been accustomed to give private performances to a paying audience until they were suppressed for scurrility. Though this had happened as far back as 1589, the memory of it may have remained fresh in the minds of the neighbouring residents, and they successfully petitioned the Council against the establishment of a professional theatre in their midst, so that Burbage was

161

refused permission after all, and his family were left with the
building on their hands.

It was not for long, however. Times were changing; the
queen was not moving about so frequently from palace to
palace as she had done when she was young, and Westminster
was becoming the regular headquarters of the Court. More
and more officials and courtiers found it worth while to have
town-houses there, building and development went on in
the space between the two cities of Westminster and London,
and a new demand for theatrical entertainment made itself
felt. The former Young Men of the Inns of Court, who had
gone to the Theatre and the Curtain in their undergraduate
days, were now middle-aged and more, but were ready
enough to take pleasure in a playhouse if they could find one
to their liking, preferably on their own side of the river.
The world of Bankside was the world of other entertainments, not all of them decorous, in addition to those
provided by the theatres, and a small, select playhouse, in
a respectable neighbourhood, was just what these elderly and
cultivated playgoers required. The Blackfriars theatre could
open again and find patronage instead of disapproval.

And for this new type of audience a new type of play had
to be provided. Sound and action were important still, but
they were directed less to the emotions and more to the
mind. The largely mercantile population of London Wall
and that neighbourhood had taken pleasure in plays based
on the books it read—history books, for the most part—
and on the situations it knew and understood, such as the
difficult relations between father and son, or the problem
in business ethics that was aroused by the story of thr
Merchant of Venice. Now, however, the position had
changed, and the players and their resident playwright had
to take that change into consideration.

In the old *Henry VI* days the incidents had had to come
thick and fast, with the accompaniment of ringing declamation; it had been the same, to some extent, with *Romeo
and Juliet* and the plays that followed it. The one exception
had been *Love's Labour's Lost,* the first of all, and we have
seen already that that play had been thought suitable for a
special occasion and a special audience that was prepared,

and qualified, to *listen* to a play and appreciate the words without demanding anything much in the way of action. That sort of play was likely, then, to appeal to the new theatre-public that was arising, but it must be borne in mind that that public had been brought up, in its younger days, on the old melodramatic fare of Kyd's *Spanish Tragedy* and the original crude versions of the tales of Hamlet and King Lear. There would have to be some sort of compromise, with a discreet combination of incident and intellect, if the players were to satisfy the judicious audiences at the new indoor theatre, and at the same time the new plays had better not be written for that theatre alone. They would be more warmly welcomed, and more profitably attended, if they could be made to appeal in turn to the larger audiences at the Globe. A successful example of this is the construction of *Julius Caesar*. The episode of violent, murderous action, which everybody knew about and would consequently expect, comes in the exact middle of the play, and the whole first part is devoted to a presentation of the general conditions and personal reactions that led up to it. These have been made so lifelike and interesting that the audience is eager to stay on and see, through two more acts and a half, what came of it all and what happened to the people who had been involved in it and the city-state in which it had come to pass. For those who liked emotional declamation, there had been in the first few minutes a passionate speech by a subordinate character who did not appear again, and this had served at the same time to indicate the general feelings in Rome before the main personage appeared. After that, the audience in general, and the thinking audience in particular, would be ready to listen to the conversation of Cassius, and appreciate the pains he takes to justify the conspiracy against Caesar by persuading Brutus to take part in it. The play's fascination lies not only in what the characters do, but more and more in what they say, what they think, and consequently, what they are.

In another play of this period the author seems to have been carried away this new fascination, to the detriment of the drama. *Troilus and Cressida* begins with a trumpet-tongued prologue and a couple of briskly conversational scenes involving some love-poetry of considerable beauty, some smart, cynical back-chat, and a parade of warriors in armour returning from the battlefield. Then, by way of contrast and surprise, comes a scene that is almost entirely static, wherein Agamemnon and his fellow-commanders hold a council of war. Like a very similar scene in Shaw's *Saint Joan,* it commands unremitting attention, since it is devoted to a straightforward exposition of the recent progress of the war, the present deadlock and the attitude of the Greeks to their reverses. Agamemnon regards them as necessary trials, the aged Nestor corroborates him with an additional opinion that these tests will clear away the less efficient of their allies and leave the nucleus with all the more strength to recover itself, Menelaus says nothing at all, and the field is clear for the observations of Ulysses.

And here, quite possibly, is the rock on which the fortunes of the play originally split. Tactfully, guilefully and with unhesitating accuracy he˙ undermines their complacent acceptance of the position, and sums up the whole with the blunt conclusion that

> to end a tale of length,
> Troy in our weakness stands, not in her strength.

It is an immense and magnificent speech, with its imagery drawn from the solar system (even though it reprehensibly calls the sun a planet), its insistence on order and degree and its terrifying picture of the results of anarchy. Shakespeare must have enjoyed writing it, actors must enjoy speaking it, audiences will thoroughly enjoy listening to it, if it is well and intelligently spoken, but, beyond all question, it calls for a first-rate actor.

Nor is that all. Agamemnon accepts the diagnosis of his army's 'sickness' and asks for advice about a remedy, and Ulysses begins the answer with a speech not quite so long as the last, but quite different and very, very funny. He describes Achilles sulking in his tent and ridiculing the generals, while Patroclus gives imitations of them for his diversion. It is with a certain relish that Ulysses describes Patroclus imitating Agamemnon and Nestor in succession (particularly to an audience that includes both Nestor and

Agamemnon) and concludes with an impression of a
old gentleman hurriedly putting on armour in the
Nestor manages to change the subject by pointing
other people, particularly Ajax, are going the same
due course, when Aeneas has interrupted the discussion by
coming from Troy with Hector's challenge to a friendly
combat in the true spirit of chivalry. Ulysses turns this to
good account by suggesting that Ajax, not Achilles, should
be selected as the Greek champion. Should Hector win, the
defeat of Ajax would not be such a blow to morale as that
of Achilles, while if the victory should to go Ajax, it would
give Achilles the set-down he obviously needs. The act is
ended, Ulysses has had a magnificent opportunity to establish himself in the eyes and ears of the audience, and Hector
has not yet appeared at all.

At this point, if there had been any idea that the star
part was going to be Hector's, it must have gone by the
board. Hector is a heroic figure, he has some noble things
to say, and a brutal, tragic death-scene, but it is hardly
imaginable that Burbage would have been cast for this
when the author was writing a far larger part full of guile,
wit and fascination. The young soldier-heroes have had their
day; now the author is constructing a character more
ingenious and unscrupulous than any since Richard III,
but sympathetic as Richard III was not, since in this play
his duplicity and worldly-wisdom are exercised not in his own
interests but in those of the cause and the general whom he
serves. Ulysses has two or three more scenes of some importance, one including the great speech beginning, 'Time hath,
my lord, a wallet at his back', after Achilles, at Ulysses's
own suggestion, has been deliberately ignored by Agamemnon and his colleagues, but after his hurried announcement,
in the heat of the battle, that the great Achilles is at last
arming to take the field again, we see and hear of him no
more.

This curious construction, which amounts to a changing
of horses in mid-stream, is surely responsible for the neglect
of the play until very recent times. Audiences might well
have expected to see Burbage as Hector, a straight development from his other princely parts. What they saw was a

development of his recent performance as Brutus, with a strong touch of his old Richard III intelligence, but nothing much came of it, and he faded out before the end. Hector had been long in appearing and effective in his few speeches and combats, but he was not Burbage. Then he, too, passed out of sight, and still the play went on. The last figure to hold the stage was Troilus, who had opened the play, and was now seen, and heard, rallying his followers in the true spirit of Hector and putting his own personal tragedy behind him in the greater cause of Troy. His development from petulant lover to 'a second hope, as fairly built as Hector', is a fine theme, but the hard fact is that Burbage was too old to play him, and in a supporting part Burbage could not help being the more interesting of the two. It is the old *Romeo and Juliet* problem over again, and this time it must have been insurmountable.

The evidence—what there is of it—suggests very strongly that the play was an embarrassing failure. It appears in the Stationers' Register in February 1603 as licensed for printing when the publisher had 'gotten sufficient aucthority for yt', but it was not published until 1609. A second impression, in the same year, stated roundly in a preface that if the 'grand possessors' had had their way it would not have been published at all, and that the general public had not had the chance to see it. The pagination of the First Folio shows that it was very nearly left out of that collection, being put in as an afterthought between the Histories and the Tragedies, and it is clear that in some people's minds, in Jacobean days, it was an unfortunate experiment about which the less said the better.

There is a point here that may help us in dating the play. The difficulty of equating the contemplative and dynamic elements had already cropped up in *Julius Caesar,* produced in 1599, where the player of the conscientious, thoughtful Brutus has to use all his personality and attractiveness if he is not to seem a dull dog when contrasted with the flamboyant Antony. Irving's appreciation of this point is shown by his answer to Ellen Terry when she suggested he should put on the play and appear as Brutus. 'That is the part for the actor because it needs acting, but the actor-manager's part is

Anthony—Anthony scores all along the line. Now, when the actor and actor-manager fight in a play and when there's no part in it for you, I think it's wise to leave it alone.'[1]

With an actor like Burbage, fresh from a series of comparatively youthful parts, the difficulty might have been less apparent (particularly if we remember that historically Brutus was a younger man than Cassius), and Shakespeare may have overlooked it until it made itself felt in the performance of another play. Put *Troilus and Cressida* between *Julius Caesar* and *Hamlet*, and we get an unexpectedly coherent sequence. Not only does Polonius refer to having played Julius Caesar at the university, which would be a topical joke if Shakespeare's *Caesar* were a recent production, the parts of Caesar and Polonius being traditionally played by the same actor (known as the First Old Man) in any stock company, but the king's admission to the queen about the hurried burial of Polonius carries distinct and almost certainly unconscious echoes of a similar passage in Plutarch's life of Julius Caesar as translated by North. Moreover, the long passage between Hamlet and the First Player about a recent play on the story of Troy, unpopular in performance and acted 'not above once', takes on a new significance if it is accepted as a wry allusion to a fairly recent fiasco, and an apology on the author's part for having failed to please. The extracts spoken by Hamlet and the Player have the true *Troilus* ring, and one line occurs that is taken almost word for word from a remark by Troilus about the 'fan and wind' of Hector's sword. The echoes and allusions are too many and too significant to be written off as merely coincidental. It has been maintained elsewhere that the internal evidence indicates a date of 1600 for *Hamlet* rather than the too easily accepted 1601. This gives us a logical sequence of development and construction. Brutus is a thinker's part, and runs the risk of being overtopped by Antony. Ulysses is a thinker's part, and himself overtops Hector, upsetting the balance of the play by doing so. Hamlet, the most fascinating thinker of them all, is balanced

[1]Laurence Irving, *Henry Irving; the Actor and his World* (Faber & Faber, 1951), p. 499.

by three men of his own age, all contrasted with himself and with each other, and in his sudden confrontation with Laertes in the graveyard he shows himself able to overtop them all. The Burbage voice may not be able to out-bellow the extravagances of Laertes, but the Burbage gift of terrifying intensity and *static* passion, as in his interruption of that other funeral in *Richard III*, can dominate the beholders on the stage and off it. It is only the botchers-up of the First Quarto, compiled for a Hamlet with less subtlety but more taste for fustian, who have made him leap into the grave along with Laertes and the beloved dead. From the Folio text we can imagine that his appearance has created a stunned tableau; for a moment the king and his court stand, in Hamlet's own phrase, 'like wonder-wounded hearers', and then Laertes is out of the grave and at Hamlet's throat.

And, for the first time, we are conscious of Hamlet's physical strength. Those lines of his call for quiet, almost leisured speaking, with their piled-up consonants and sibilants on the tongue. They are not the words of a man half-choked or struggling, but of one who is in command of the situation, and knows it. If poured out in a hurry, they will be little more than spluttering, but, as with Richard's lines to the halberdier, their very deliberation makes them terrible. The fingers of Hamlet on his opponent's wrists are stronger and more inexorable than those of Laertes, and potentially crueller as well, and the effect of that pain, frustration and humiliation on Laertes, who had so lately come near to being chosen king by a cheering multitude, but now has to be rescued and spared at the petition of the queen, is such that for the rest of the scene he never speaks again. When they are parted, there is no need for Hamlet to be passionate to Horatio or the queen. Indeed, the lines beginning 'I loved Ophelia' carry much more weight if they come out as a sincere explanation of his behaviour. In the same way, when he turns to Laertes there is no need for vocal extravagance; there is much more scorn and contempt in the words if they are brought out with full appreciation of their sensationalism and consequent absurdity, and in a moment he has abandoned even that. He speaks to Laertes courteously, almost apologetically—remember, he still has no idea just how Ophelia died, or what Laertes thinks *he* had to do with it— and when silently rebuffed he accepts the rejection with a regretful couplet—once again a sign of a return to polite formalism—and takes himself away.

It is the fact of contrast, not contest, that has been so impressive here, as it is throughout. Fortinbras, the man of action, Laertes, the man of passion, Horatio, the scholar and observer, move around Hamlet and, like Ulysses's planets, 'observe degree, priority and place', their actions and reactions preserving a quality of balance that yet seems purely natural and makes the play the masterpiece it is. Here, above all other plays in the Shakespearean canon, the poet and the player have met in the happiest conjunction, not by mere chance, but by the continued, conscientious consideration and practice of their art.

There is a small but interesting feature that may be noticed at this period of the turn of the century in general and the great tragedies in particular. Shakespeare's keen musical sense is leading him on to more elaborate vocal ensembles, as in the spoken quintet in which Ulysses and Troilus observe Cressida's temptation by Diomed and her reluctant surrender, while Thersites comments on it in his own coarse fashion. The main melody, so to speak, is carried on by Diomed and Cressida, dropping to a whisper or an expressive silence when the observers have to speak, but never coming to a full close. When either of them is heard again, it is with an echo of what was last said, so that there is no sense of the commentary having interrupted the flow. The end comes with the departure of Diomed, three regretful couplets by Cressida as she goes back into the tent, and an unpleasant remark by Thersites; the silence that follows is eloquent in itself, to be broken at last by the gentle hint of Ulysses, 'All's done, my lord' and its stunned and desolate acknowledgement from a Troilus who cannot yet bring himself to admit full consciousness of what he has seen and heard.

The whole episode is a *tour-de-force* of writing, and calls for great precision of timing on the part of the players. It may well have involved so much trouble in rehearsing, and have not been successful enough in performance, for the author to have considered it not worth while to do again in so elaborate a form. A simplified version occurs in the fourth act of *Othello,* where Iago leads Cassio on to talk and laugh about the courtesan Bianca, while the jealous Othello over-hears only part of their conversation, and later in the same act when Othello is reading the despatches from Venice and his indignant exclamations show that he is at the same time listening to the conversation between his wife and the envoy Lodovico.

Elsewhere the method is even simpler still. The first words of Laertes to the priest at Ophelia's funeral draw forth a comment from Hamlet to Horatio as they watch the ceremony unobserved, and when the attention of the audience has to be brought back to the main group, Laertes is made to repeat his query, 'What ceremony else?' in order to keep up the continuity and importance of the priest's answer. Similarly, in *Macbeth,* when the stage is crowded with figures on the discovery of the murder of Duncan, interest has to be shifted momentarily to the king's two sons, who share the general alarm and indignation, but must be allowed in addition to express the personal apprehensions that separate them from the rest. Their hurried exchanges come when the cry of 'Look to the lady' has drawn the attention of the others to the collapse of Lady Macbeth, and it is the repetition of those same words, though by another character and in another tone—for it is part of a general recommendation to everyone—that calls the general company to mind and serves to get them off the stage and leave Malcolm and Donalbain to arrange their hurried flight.

By this time, too, there was another factor to be con-sidered. Shakespeare was past his first youth, and Burbage was only a few years younger, and this inevitably influenced the development of the mind of the one and the body of the other. Shakespeare turned more and more to creating contemplative parts, and Burbage to playing them, and the conditions of the Blackfriars theatre were particularly favourable to both. *Othello* has all the characteristics of a play written for such a house, where a small, intimate audience can hear every word without having to be assailed

with loud declamation. The passionate outcries of Othello
in his agony of doubt and disillusion are the more terrifying
because they are *not* the accepted convention of the place,
but stand out disturbingly against the conversation and
naturalism of the other characters. They emphasise the
isolation and loneliness of the Moor (a blackamoor, let us
remember, not the tawny Arabian whom he himself would
call a Turk) in an alien environment with which he has been
able to cope till now, and which has hitherto found him
'all-in-all sufficient'. His roaring, ringing tones are quite
unlike the lines that Shakespeare ordinarily wrote for
Burbage, and it may be questioned whether this part was
in fact written for him to play.

Its music is that of Pistol imitating Alleyn, or of a part
like Titus, written for Alleyn in the old days, and there are
reasonable grounds for the thinking that it was in fact
written to Alleyn's measure, for some occasion when the
Admiral's Men and the Chamberlain's Men were required
to give a joint performance. The play is another two-part
one; the man who feels and suffers, and cries out in his
agony, being set against the man who thinks and comments
in the coldest of cold blood, who expresses himself in casual-
sounding conversation and whose last word, when faced with
the prospect of a slow death in torment, is a vow of eternal
silence. The original Hieronymo of the every-popular *Spanish
Tragedy*, Shakespeare's original Titus, Marlowe's original
Tamburlaine, is balanced against the original Richard III,
each is given a free hand to play the other off the stage—
if he can do it—and the play is so ingeniously constructed
that it does not suffer for it.

At first, Iago has it all his own way, particularly in the
intimate conditions at Court or Blackfriars, where he has
the audience within easy reach of his conversational tones,
and can utter the most outrageous sentiments in a calm and
matter-of-fact way that makes them all the more appalling
to listen to. When he is shouting obscenities under Brabantio's
window at the beginning, there is no music in them, there are
biting consonants rather than ringing vowels; the effect, as
he expressly intends it to be, is something like the jarring
horror of a fire-alarm—and the dwellers in timber-built

Elizabethan London knew well enough what *that* meant! Othello's utterances, by contrast, are full of calm dignity, whether he is checking a potential street-brawl in its inception, justifying his courtship before an emergency meeting of the Venetian Senate, or even reprimanding and dismissing an officer for being drunk on duty. The lines flow with the ease of great and quiet strength, but at the central point of the play, when Iago's hints and suggestions disturb the confidence that has upheld Othello hitherto, the flow changes to a torrent like the Pontic sea that he so passionately describes. The 1622 quarto of the play specifies that it 'hath beene diverse times acted at the Globe, and at the Black Friers, by his Maiesties Seruants', and we may reasonably assume that Burbage took over Othello's part in the company's own theatre, where there would be no question of co-operation with Alleyn and his colleagues, and less of the intimacy that a small theatre contributes to the hints, whisperings and cruel, damaging comments that are the essence of Iago. Burbage may well have played Othello and been deservedly applauded, but that does not necessarily mean that the part suited him any more than, nearly three centuries later, it suited Irving.

The use of rhyme in this play is effective in giving an air of decorous artificiality when required, as it was in *Richard II*, to avoid the embarrassment of too much or too violent personal opinion. The Doge of Venice speaks in deliberately sententious couplets when urging Brabantio to make the best of a bad business; Brabantio answers him in kind, with four bitter couplets of his own, and shows what he thinks of the effort by pointedly breaking into prose and moving that they get on with the official business of the meeting. In the later scene of the landing in Cyprus, the gentle raillery of Desdemona's prose is met by the epigrammatic rhymes with which Iago answers her, culminating in his longer passage enumerating the qualities of a virtuous woman and summarising them in an uncomplimentary line that Desdemona laughs off as a 'lame and impotent conclusion'. Behind it all, as in the earlier play, there lies the continuous sense that the speakers are conversing in public, or at least in the hearing of others, and must take some heed of what they say in the circumstances.

Another example of this occurs in *All's Well that Ends Well,* when Helena makes her appearance in the Court of France. Burbage's part here must obviously have been the king. By this time he would be getting on for 40, and Shakespeare is making allowance for the fact in the ages he is ascribing to his principal characters. Hamlet is said categorically to be 30, Iago a hardened and experienced 28, Othello goes so far as to describe himself as 'declin'd into the vale of years', and rubs it in by hurriedly adding 'though that's not much' as if he were reluctant to admit it at all. The King of France, in this play, is old enough to speak as the contemporary of Bertram's dead father, underlining it by the slow, dragging bitterness of the words

> He lasted long
> But on us both did haggish age steal on
> And wore us out of act.

He must, then, be regarded by everyone as being well past middle age, though younger than the bluff old courtier Lafeu. In sickness and in health alike he moves and speaks with a grave authority that makes him the centre of the stage whenever he is on it, so that he takes unquestioned charge of the successive dramatic tensions of the last scene.

This calls for careful handling of the scene in which Helena claims to be allowed to treat him for his infirmity. Disillusioned and in pain, he has given up hope, and answers her with a flat but courteous refusal, and at first sight it seems that she, and the author, are at a deadlock. How, in all decorum and plausibility, is one to go on from there? The anwer is, then and now, to avoid direct contradiction and turn the conversation into an apparently objective discussion. The king has ended his refusal with a polite couplet that has an air of finality about it, but gives a chance for an acknowledgement on Helena's part, if only of acceptance and regret. What it gets is a couplet, indeed, but not so much an acceptance as a comment, though a very polite and respectful one, indicating that it is the king's own fault if he refuses even to consider treatment. This in turn is followed by a still respectful reminder that such things, after all, have happened before. The king is tempted, in spite of himself, to go on listening, but determines firmly against it, adding a hint that if the enquirer is hoping for a fee, she will get thanks but no money for her trouble. This brings her to a sharper insistence that it is knowledge, not personal skill, that she is putting at his disposal, and that her own part in it is negligible. Involuntarily he is led on to question after question—how long the treatment would take, and how much she is prepared to stake on her success. Before he knows where he is, he has accepted her challenge, with her own reputation and life staked as the price of failure, and has promised her, if she succeeds, the husband of her choice from among the Royal Wards—young people of good family and estate, but fatherless, and disposable in marriage at the king's discretion. Helena has gained her point, and talked the king round, largely by the avoidance of special pleading or undue emotionalism. As in the first scene of *Richard II,* the use of rhyme does much to show that the proper formalities are being observed, but in this scene the matter is one concerned with cool, logical reason instead of passionate accusation and defence. An application is made, through the proper channels and backed by reasonable arguments; there is no disconcerting attempt to cross the boundaries of etiquette, or exercise any emotional blackmail, in the way it is presented, and there seems to be no reason, after all, why it should not be granted. That, even now, is one way of getting what one wants out of a public official or a Government department, which may find a refusal more difficult to justify than acceptance, if application has been made throughout in the appropriate form.

Another point worth considering is the effect, on the play in general, and this scene in particular, of giving the king's part to an actor of the status and capacity of Burbage. The vulgar charge of husband-hunting and opportunism, sometimes preferred against Helena, falls completely flat if the king is presented as a person whose restoration to health is of tremendous importance to the court, to the nation, and to mankind. There have been suggestions of this from Lafeu in the first few moments of the play, and even more in Helena's later scene with the Countess, where she talks of going to Paris. For all her frank admission that it was the

thought of Bertram that had put it into her head, it is clear
that the project has at the heart of it a nobler aim, and that
for the sake of her king's health and her father's reputation
she must go to Paris, very much as Joan of Arc went to
Chinon, for greater purposes than her own. When she meets
her sovereign face to face, it is clear to her, and can be made
as clear to the spectators, that here is a person who matters
more than Bertram or anyone else whom they have seen, and
whose cure is, and must be, the first consideration of all
concerned.

When that cure is achieved, and the eligible bachelors
under the king's guardianship are paraded for her to take
her choice, she turns to rhyme again, examining and rejecting
each, to their obvious disappointment, with a charming
compliment, until she comes to Bertram. Then her tone
changes, her rhyme forsakes wit for quiet sincerity, and
her choice is made by an extra line, without a rhyme in it,
in which she tells the king, quite simply, 'This is the man'.
Bertram's indignant rejection of her, and the king's
insistence, are passionately personal, and are unrhymed,
and the king returns to rhyming couplets only when he
has moved from immediate anger to reasoned, patient
explanation of what ought to have been obvious to Bertram,
were he not so young and callow. Like the Doge's words
to Brabantio, the cadences come out with a steadying effect,
and prevent the young man from making an exhibition of
himself by further insubordination. More subtly, the passage
has another effect, of which we are barely conscious. These
are no longer the words of an ageing invalid. Helena's
treatment has indeed restored the king to health, energy
and the full exercise of his power, so that instead of being
a weary onlooker, as at his first appearance, he is in full
command of his faculties, and can speak to Bertram with
treble authority, not only as his sovereign, but as his official
guardian and his father's friend. All the same, this tolerance
and consideration have their limits. When Bertram is still
obstinate, courtly rhyme gives place to a tone of stern
rebuke that shakes the young man out of his defiance and
ends with a peremptory command, 'Speak!—thine answer?'
That answer can be nothing but apology and compliance.

It is given, though with an excess of humility that itself verges on the disrespectful, and there is no more rhyme till the king's concluding couplet marks the end of the episode, and after a long passage of prose an exchange of similar couplets between Bertram and Parolles brings the scene to a close in the usual way.

The maturity of the whole conception undermines the easy assumption that the rhymed couplets are signs of an early date. Shakespeare could rhyme like that, it is true, in his early days with the Admiral's Men—the conversation of the Talbots in *I Henry VI* shows as much—but he could not think out a situation, and draw a character in three dimensions, as he does here. It has been stated categorically, by Bernard Shaw and others, that the play was never performed in its author's lifetime, but this is contradicted by the explicit statement, in the preface to the First Folio, that all the plays in that collection have stood the test of public performance. Moreover, play-titles were unquestionably variable in Shakespeare's time, and in May 1613 the company was paid £40, with an extra bonus of £20, for presenting six plays, including 'one playe called A bad beginninge makes a good endinge', which unquestionably sounds like this one, especially as two others of the six are 'One other The Hotspur, And one other called Benedicte and Betteris', obviously *I Henry IV* and *Much Ado about Nothing* appearing under unfamiliar names.

Those performances were at Court, and the play is one which might well find its readiest and most appreciative welcome from such an audience, since its action, interest and atmosphere are those of the great country-house, the Royal Household, and the officers' mess. The local Great Lady is seen in her house at Roussillon, with her steward, her lady-in-waiting, and her comic odd-job-man—not, surely, a professional fool, but a yokel being trained with difficulty in the niceties of polite service, like Diggory in *She Stoops to Conquer*, or the well-meaning but oafish William in Hollyband's *French Schoolemaster,* who can never remember to serve bread properly on a trencher, but persists in bringing it to table in his hand.[1] The king's court at the Louvre shows

[1] M. St. Clare Byrne, *The Elizabethan Home* (Methuen, 1949), p. 24.

us courtiers old and young, those who go abroad for a season to lend a hand in a neighbouring war almost as a sporting venture, those who are kept at home because they are royal wards, too young and, for the sake of their marriage possibilities, too valuable to be let loose on such dangerous pursuits, and in Parolles a fine specimen of the genus hanger-on, acting as patronising parasite to a well-to-do young man, to whom his companionship and influence are not doing any good. All this would be entertaining to Whitehall and Blackfriars audiences because they were used to it, and interesting to Globe audiences because they were not. To the first it was a shrewd picture of contemporary society as they knew it, to the second it was a story of Goings-on in High Life, and both would enjoy it, though for widely different reasons.

This being so, there would be no reason why the poet should not repeat the process the other way round, and write a Bankside play that might also be enjoyed at Court, turning on the same joke, summed up in the proverb that at night all cats are grey. The theme of lechery frustrated has always been a diverting one. Hroswitha of Gandersheim had handled it in the 10th century with her presentation of the amorous Roman persecutor, miraculously misdirected when visiting captive Christian girls by night, kissing saucepans in the kitchen, caressing their rotundity and covering himself with lamp-black so that his own servants, and his wife, fail to recognise him when he gets home. This time the joke is against the combination of ill-intention and inexperience. Bertram fails to tell one young woman from another in the dark because in fact he has never before indulged in such an adventure, and lands himself in deeper and deeper difficulty by thinking he has done wrong by a young Florentine when in fact he has been doing right by his own neglected wife. King James's court would regard such a situation with high glee. So might Bankside audiences, particularly if they were given a different figure to laugh at, in a more familiar setting, and that was what Shakespeare provided for them when he wrote *Measure for Measure*. Here it is not the unfledged amorist but the puritanical kill-joy who is landed in the same situation and prevented,

by his lack of any means of comparison, from knowing that
he is involved with the wrong lady.

The puritan Angelo is now considered to be the leading
male part, presumably because of its two strong scenes with
the leading lady, but in the days when Isabella was played
by a talented boy, not an established actress, the balance of
the play was rather different. Angelo does not appear at all
in the third act, and has only one short scene in the fourth,
and that is not the way for an author to treat his leading
actor and chief shareholder in the company. From playing
the king of France it is a short step to playing the duke of
Vienna, and here we find a part giving Burbage occasion to
move through every act of the play, observing and influenc-
ing the action, and to employ on occasions the versatility
which audiences by this time were ready, and entitled, to
expect from him.

The anonymity of a friar's habit is in itself a very effective
disguise, and in fact his only conversation with anyone
familiar with him in his true capacity is his very short talk
with Escalus at the end of the third act. Here, by the way,
Shakespeare puts in a useful safeguard by making the
supposed friar describe himself as 'not of this country'
though at the moment on a special mission from the Holy
See. There is no change of spelling, to indicate a foreign
accent, as there would be in a designedly comic part; but
there is every justification for a slowing-down of pace, a
careful deliberation in his choice of words, that betokens
a man taking care to express himself correctly in a foreign
language, and is very different from the duke's conversation
in the earlier scenes. It takes a leading actor, also, to command a situation and reveal himself as a person of supreme
authority by the mere pulling-back of a hood. A friar's frock
is not easily removable in a hurry, and he will get no help,
therefore, from the revelation of what he is wearing under-
neath. He has to work the change by the look and carriage
of his head and shoulders alone, and by the sudden dignity
and sonority of the words put into his mouth.

His first line has a certain grim humour, which runs
through his next observations to Lucio, but the full organ-
notes come out in his words to Escalus and, still more, to

the shocked and humiliated Angelo. It is when he addresses Isabella that the note of kindness creeps in again, only to be eclipsed at the return and condemnation of Angelo to share Claudio's supposed fate. There is no indication that he had expected Mariana to intercede for her newly-married husband, still less that she would call upon Isabella to second her. He has no way of knowing just what Isabella will do, and can only repeat the logical, inexorable argument, 'He dies for Claudio's death', and wait, as uncertain as any of them, to see what happens.

What does happen is one of Shakespeare's extraordinarily dramatic silences, broken not by words but by a movement. Isabella has made up her mind, and in her turn she kneels before him to ask not for vengeance, not even for strict, impartial justice, but for mercy and a pardon. Her speech upsets his original resolution to execute Angelo and give her 'comfort of despair' by the unexpected restoration of her brother. He has to rearrange his ideas, and plays for time by changing the subject, abruptly charging the Provost with irregularity and ordering him to fetch the other condemned criminal. The eyes and the attention of the audience, and of the characters on the stage, will naturally follow the officer as he goes, and one might expect an awkward stage wait here, as it would seem that matters can make no further progress till he comes back with his prisoner. But it is in such a time of waiting that a man may speak to another, without breaking the tension or disturbing his fellows, of something relevant that is on his mind, and while practically everyone else is watching for the returning Provost, Escalus takes the opportunity to speak a few words of kindness and courtesy to his old colleague, suddenly disgraced and under sentence of death. The little exchange gives us a momentary glimpse of both men at their best, before the arrival of the Provost, with Barnardine and the still-hooded Claudio, sets the action rapidly moving on.

And, once again, the vocal versatility of Burbage is called into play. He is all gravity and authority in his charge to Barnardine, then there is a relaxation and a smile in his choice of words as he pronounces Claudio's pardon. What everyone would expect in those days, and what they would

see as a matter of course, is the sight of brother and sister
at once on their knees before the duke, too full of thankful-
ness for speech, and probably trying to kiss his hands. The
act would unite the three of them, for a few seconds, in an
intimacy cut off from the other characters and would give
him a chance to say quite quietly, as he raises her, the lines
that sound so awkward and unlikely when they are declaimed
in public:

> and for your lovely sake
> Give me your hand and say you will be mine,
> He is my brother too. But fitter time for that,

and he tries to get back to business, but happiness keeps
breaking in. Whatever his original intention, it is impossible
for him to condemn anybody to death after what he has
just done, said and learned to hope for, and Angelo's pardon
is pronounced in the friendliest terms. Lucio may well have
been expecting, by this, to get off scot-free himself, but he
is given a sharp fright before his extreme penalties are
remitted and he is merely made to marry a lady whose
situation has been explained, to the duke by Lucio himself,
and to Escalus by Mistress Overdone, as a seduction under
promise of marriage. His indignant descriptions of his Kate
are as natural a reaction as Bertram's about Diana in the
other play, and are very properly disregarded, and when he
protests against such a marriage as 'pressing to death, whip-
ping *and* hanging' the duke's cheerful reply is 'Slandering a
prince deserves it'. Both remarks are exaggerations, and both
the speakers know it, as Lucio, yelling in comic indignation,
is rushed off by the officers to a marriage that has a parallel
with Angelo's and Claudio's.

Escalus and the Provost are given promises of advancement, Angelo is restored to some degree of favour, and the
lines of Isabella show, by a swift change of tone and content,
that the duke is hoping to win happiness, not confidently
conferring it as a matter of course. It is a touch of humility
and humanity that prevents the play from ending on a note
of complacent self-satisfaction. Bankside must have enjoyed
it, and apparently it appealed to the politer audience as well,

since it was performed at court on Boxing Night in 1604, and would not have been selected for that important occasion unless there had been a pretty good idea that it would please. But then, king James may well have felt pleasurably complimented by the Burbage part, secure in the conviction that he was that kind of prince himself, and that everybody knew it.

Chapter Ten

THREEFOLD ECLIPSE

AT THIS POINT it may be as well to consider another voice that was being heard with increasing effect among the King's Men, as the players had now become. Kempe had left the company in 1599, and they had to get a new clown. The newcomer was Robert Armin, and though there is no specific record of the Shakespearean parts he played, there are one or two pieces of evidence that give a considerable indication of his style, and from which we may venture, perhaps, to cast him in certain Shakespearean parts.

He was a pupil of the famous Richard Tarlton, and was looked upon by some people as Tarlton's obvious successor in the same line of business. What that was, we gather from one or two pieces of contemporary evidence. Peacham's poem, already cited, about the effect of his face looking through the curtains of the tiring-house indicates that he had a personality of his own, and bears out Chambers's conclusion that his 'considerable reputation was evidently in the main that of a joyous jester and buffoon'. Sir Richard Baker, who had been a young student at the Inns of Court in Tarlton's time, published, in 1643, his *Chronicle of the Kings of England,* and among his list of men of note in Elizabeth's time pays tribute to '*Richard Bourbidge*, and *Edward Allen,* two such Actors as no age must ever look to see the like, and, to make their Comedies compleat, *Richard Tarleton* (Plate III), who for the Part called the Clowns Part, never had his match, never will have'. The old gentleman was between 70 and 80 when he wrote that, but had not given up his theatre-going, as the only two other names he mentions as noteworthy in this connection are those of Shakespeare and the comparatively modern Jonson as 'Writers of Playes, and such as had been Players themselves',

182

and his inclusion of Tarlton in such company, and in such incisive terms, must be allowed to carry weight. The well-known portrait-sketch of him (Plate III, and see Appendix, page 204), stumping along with his tabor and pipe and glancing truculently over his shoulder, gives a fair indication of his technique, and when that technique occurs in the later plays of Shakespeare we may justly assume that it was employed by Armin. Instead of dullness and pomposity we are given ʼargument, contradiction and something in the way of crusty challenge; the country simplicity of Constable Dull gives place to the cheerful indecorum of Pompey, Feste, and the clown digging Ophelia's grave. In the earlier plays, the comedian—usually Kempe—had been exhibited as dominating people of still duller wits; even Falstaff had borne himself discreetly in the presence of his unquestioned superiors until that last, fatal mistake on his young friend's coronation-day. Now, on the contrary, the picture is one of wit—sometimes extremely coarse wit—against authority. It is Feste against Malvolio, Pompey against the magistrates who are committing him, Master Lavache, in the most genial way, against the Countess, his employer, and Thersites against everybody. The pupil of Tarlton, the author of *A Nest of Ninnies,* the pamphleteer who called himself 'Clonnico del Curtanio Snuffe' when he was playing at the Curtain, and altered it to 'Clonnico del Mondo Snuffe' when the company moved to the Globe, had come cheerfully and disrespectfully into his own.

A rather crude little woodcut on the title-page of *The Two Maids of More-clacke* is generally accepted as representing Armin, and certainly shows an amount of jovial truculence that would go well with a repetition of the Tarlton technique. This being so, we may justifiably look through the later plays for parts that might have been cut to such a measure, and it is not difficult to find them.

Take, for instance, *King Lear.* We have been told often enough, and dogmatically enough, that Armin took the part of the Fool, but critical investigation shows that there is no evidence, and little likelihood, of his doing anything of the sort. Looking at the supposed portrait of Armin and the undoubted portrait of his master and prototype Tarlton, we can hardly accept the casting of this sturdy creature for the frail, whimsical character, Lear's 'pretty knave', who drifts in without introduction and is dropped out without explanation and —most significant of all—is so little essential to the drama that he could be left out of it for 100 years and more until Macready put him back into it in the 19th century. It is hard to believe that the Snuffe who wrote *Foole upon Foole* would calmly agree to being left out of the first scene

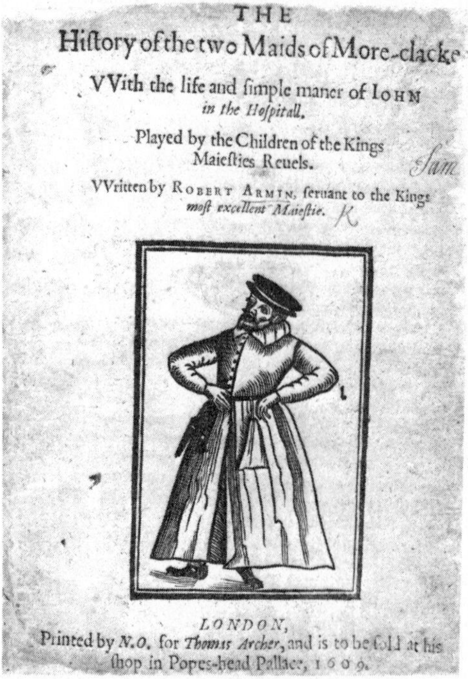

THE
Hiftory of the two Maids of More-clacke

VVith the life and simple maner of IOHN
in the Hospitall.

Played by the Children of the Kings
Maiefties Reuels.

VVritten by ROBERT ARMIN, feruant to the Kings
moft excellent Maieftie.

LONDON,
Printed by N.O. for *Thomas Archer*, and is to be fold at his
fhop in Popes-head Pallace, 1 6 0 9.

Fig. 5. Title-page of *The Two Maids of More-Clacke*, with portrait supposed to be that of Robert Armin, probably dressed as 'John in the Hospitall', the comic part specifically mentioned in the title-page.

and denied the opportunity of commenting, at that stage, on Lear's own folly in dividing his kingdom and disinheriting his daughter, especially when such opportunities for caustic criticism were not ignored by the author, but created and given to another player. In short, would the bluff, critical, argumentative Armin stand calmly by and let somebody else play Kent? The best-known remark in Shaw's *Pygmalion* surely provides the answer.

An accepted clown usually has, and sometimes displays, some one serious quality of high standard, which is often welcomed by his public as a seasoning to his buffoonery. With Grock and George Robey it was music, with Will Hay it was astronomy (though this, admittedly, was kept sternly apart from his public professional appearances), with others it may be 'straight' acting or singing. Even so, we may perceive, it was with Armin. Towards the end of his life he became a serious writer or pamphleteer, and his stage development suggests an increase in his ability to play straight parts which can still give him a chance to appear in his old line of robust and sometimes knockabout comedy. Kent's part is a glorious example of this. From the outset he is a sympathetic character, courteous and tactful in the face of Gloucester's introduction of the illegitimate Edmund, blunt and considerably less tactful in his frank criticism of his master, ending in defiance and banishment, and showing his fidelity to him by seeking service with him as soon as he has got himself satisfactorily disguised.

After that, in his new capacity of faithful but independent serving-man, he can and does let himself go. If indeed he was anything like Tarlton—and a good deal of contemporary opinion suggests that he was—the sketch of Tarlton gives a clear indication of the way in which the younger man may have played Kent, relishing the brisk rough-and-tumble in which he trips up the heels of the pompous and cowardly Oswald, and the flow of rude epithets with which he overwhelms him till he frightens him to screaming-point with a sword and is set in the stocks for it. Armin is giving the spectators a substantial touch of the old Armin whom they knew, and at the same time a sight of something they had not seen him do before, a study of the English serving-man, as devoted and disrespectful as Sam Weller was to Mr. Pickwick, until his last couplet shows that he has nothing left to live for, and he quietly prepares to follow his exacting master into the realms of death.

Just as Shakespeare seems to have followed the court story of *All's Well* with its Bankside counterpart in *Measure for Measure*, so in *Timon of Athens* the Globe playgoers may have seen their own version of the complacency, liberality and bitter disillusionment of Lear. A legendary king giving away his property and authority to his two elder daughters was a matter of imagination, but the sight of a nobleman spending and lending lavishly and joyfully and becoming bankrupt in consequence was something they understood from personal observation and, to some extent, personal experience. The point of realisation and disillusionment

comes at a later stage in *Timon* than it does in *Lear*, because
there is less point in showing what Lear did with his kingship
while he enjoyed it than there is in showing what Timon did
with his money. Lear's royalty has to be taken for granted,
Timon's nobility has to be illustrated, not so much by his
actions, which are unwise enough, but by the generous,
muddle-headed mind behind them. More than a century
after Shakespeare's death, audiences were still applauding
that spirit in Sheridan's Charles Surface and Goldsmith's
Good-natured Man—and anyone who had dealings with
Sheridan or Goldsmith had every reason to know about
unpaid bills in fact as well as fiction.

As Lear is confronted with the disguised Kent, so Burbage's Timon is subjected from the outset to the caustic
tongue of Armin in the person of Apemantus the philosopher.
If we look at the Tarlton-Armin pictures and then at the
lines of Apemantus, we can see what an effective sparring-
partner the philosopher makes to the man who had played
jovial, kindly princes and could put on at will, by this time,
'that in his countenance that a man would fain call master'.
It is his own personal servants, the men who *have* called
him master, who have little thought for their unpaid wages,
but think kindly of him when he can no longer afford to
pay them, nor they afford to serve him unpaid. It is those
at a greater remove, the tradesmen who know him only as
an unsatisfactory customer and the acquaintances who have
looked on him as an inexhaustible source of miscellaneous
gifts, loans and hospitality, who feel justly indignant when
he has to be written off as a bad debt, or unjustly resentful
when he in his turn resorts to them for help.

There would be many of both sorts to be met with in the
fast life of Bankside and the Liberties of the Clink. For
Globe audiences in general, King Lear might be a person in
history, but Lord Timon—as the characters often call him—
was someone much more easily imaginable, like my lord This
or Sir Henry That, who had run through his father's fortune
and then his wife's, and was now faced with an enforced
retirement unless he could make a fantastic recovery by
betting on the bears. And, at the end of it all, there is a
note of encouragement and consolation. Lear shivering in

the storm, and Timon digging roots in the wilderness, each goes through an ordeal of degradation and hopelessness, and comes out the better for it, even though it has broken him utterly so that there is nothing left but death. Yet even so, there are some, like the banditti, who find themselves, almost reluctantly, a little better for having known him; and Alcibiades, the one former friend who is really anxious to help him in his poverty, though he can least afford to do so, at last marches against Athens in support of him, able to 'use the olive with his sword' in the strength of the new-found gold that Timon has uncovered and disdained. There may well have been feelings like that, and people like that, among the human wreckage on the South Bank, and the local theatre audiences would be none the worse for being encouraged to think so when Shakespeare and Burbage showed them the way.

It is when an actor is at the height of his success, and is acclaimed for it, that he can afford to depict failure, and with Burbage at the height of his development and fame, Shakespeare could safely write a part for him, at some remove a sequel to *Julius Caesar,* in which he could show what eventually happened to Antony. It is in his life of Mark Antony that Plutarch tells his version of the story of Timon, and it looks as if Shakespeare had come across this in the course of his reading and thinking about the later, greater play. Here, too, there is a part for Armin in the character of Enobarbus, as critical as Apemantus and nearly as faithful as Kent—so nearly that we feel a pang of pity when we see him not quite able to stay faithful to the end, and can readily believe that after this one act of yielding to expediency he will never know a happy moment again.

Vocally speaking, Antony's part is a most interesting example of Shakespare's craftsmanship. Burbage's part in the earlier play was assuredly Brutus; when the two plays are performed in close succession, and the same actor plays Antony in both, the casting is inclined to throw *Julius Caesar* somewhat out of balance. Antony the demagogue, stirring up Rome to mutiny in one of the most famous pieces of declamation Shakespeare ever wrote, calls for a flamboyance and a quality of vocal resonance that were not in Burbage's capacity. On the other hand, with the build-up that the earlier play had given him, and the occasional *short* bursts that recall the eloquence of the earlier, younger man, Shakespeare has contrived for Burbage a moving study of that former Antony now grown old and less resilient than he has been. The contrast is deliberate, and is underlined in the text, not only in allusions to the grey which is beginning to mingle with 'the younger brown' in his hair, but explicitly in the words of one of his messages to Octavius Caesar, whom he charges with being

> Proud and disdainful, harping on what I am,
> Not what he knew I was.

A few lines earlier in the same scene he has cried

> Now gods and devils!
> Authority melts from me: of late, when I cried 'Ho!'
> Like boys unto a muss, kings would start forth
> And cry 'Your will?' Have you no ears? I am
> Antony yet.

So he is, but only for a few moments at a time. He can no longer keep it up continually, and knows it. He has reached, and passed, the highest point of worldly achievement, and is now on the way downhill. Though the lines embody the tragedy of a man who has consciously passed that peak, they could only have been written for a man who had not yet come to it. Had that period of decline really arrived for Burbage, or even come into view, Shakespeare would never have written the lines for him, not necessarily from compassion, but from common-sense. Hamlet's advice to the Players shows that. Any device of action, exaggeration or similarity of circumstance that can attract the audiences to the personality of the actor rather than the character he portrays is to be avoided, especially if 'some necessary question of the play be then to be considered', and the spectators can be as easily distracted by pitying the ageing player as they might be by unseasonable laughing at the clown.

With regard to Cleopatra, the position is rather different. For the boy who played her, advancing age did not mean

the end of his career, but the change from one stage of it
to the next. Cleopatra can make, and does make, numerous
allusions to her age, her wrinkles and even, now and then,
her experience with Julius Caesar before Antony, and
Pompey the Great before either of them. She is never, in
fact, given a love-scene that she is obviously too old to play;
we are insidiously persuaded of her spell over Antony by
the way people talk about it, so that we find ourselves taking
it for granted and not realising that on almost every occasion
when we see them together they are either passionately
quarrelling or while Antony is helplessly enslaved Cleopatra
is teasing him in an almost Congrevian style, and showing
herself as merciless as Millamant in *The Way of the World.*
Her own hungry passion for him is revealed to us only in
his absence or, in that magnificent last act after his death,
when the boy-actress, conscious that his voice is breaking
and his beard growing, can boldly say

> My resolution's plac'd, and I have nothing
> Of woman in me,

rising superior to his supposed womanhood as he had done,
not much earlier, when he uttered to the listening spirits
of evil the terrible prayer of Lady Macbeth.

Enobarbus, at his first appearance, follows his old line of
genial disrespect, but not for long. Cleopatra makes a sudden
appearance in something very different from her former
after-dinner mood, and he is at once decorous and obedient
in the presence of someone with whom he has no inclination
to take liberties. She is a queen, and his hostess, and he pays
her all proper respect while he is in her presence. When he
is alone with Antony it is a different matter, and he drops
into his mood of easy familiarity, playing the privileged
clown until he is momentarily shocked into sobriety by the
news of Fulvia's death. It does not last long, however, and
in a moment or two he is giving a shrewd and embarrassingly
truthful summary of the present state of things until Antony
has to stop him with a brusque veto on any more 'light
answers' and give him orders instead, showing at the same
time how much he relies on him as a genuinely efficient
subordinate.

He fraternises wittily and agreeably with the aides-de-camp of Caesar and of Sextus Pompeius, and enjoys himself uproariously at the famous drinking-party on the latter's galley. His clowning technique is a great deal subtler than Kempe's, but he keeps up his old practice of being the stern, shrewd critic of his master, and as Antony goes deeper and deeper into the morass of involvement with his two widely-differing royal ladies, Enobarbus finds more and more to criticise. After the great break with Rome, he is on very different terms with Cleopatra. She knows how much her lover needs him and depends on him, so she treats him with something very like the familiarity of an equal, and he in turn pays her the compliment of taking her seriously and telling her frankly why he disapproves of her taking an active part in the campaign, as she is doing Antony no good by it. The shrewd clown is becoming a shrewd counsellor: like Kent he tries to persuade his master not to do the wrong thing for the wrong reason, but his arguments are contemptuously dismissed, and Antony insists, against all persuasions, on fighting Caesar at sea.

The result is the catastrophe of Actium. Cleopatra's flagship takes flight, followed by her fleet of 60 sail. That is as much as Enobarbus can bear to see, and it is from Scarus that he learns that there is even worse behind. Antony himself has turned tail and fled after her, leaving his navy to shift for themselves. This desertion starts a landslide. Canidius, who has just been put in command of a land force of 19 legions and 12,000 horse, roundly announces his intention of following the example of six of the subordinate provincial kings, and going over to Caesar with the whole of his army. Enobarbus admits that this may well be the reasonable thing to do, but all the same he cannot yet bring himself to do it, and against all his blunt professions of hard-headed common-sense he still finds himself following 'the wounded chance of Antony'.

The clown is now turned serious adviser. Cleopatra consults him almost on equal terms, though she has little use for his summary of the position when she gets it. He himself stands at one side to listen to her interview with Caesar's envoy, and goes away to fetch Antony when the interview takes a rather dangerous turn, suggesting that Cleopatra herself may be contemplating the possibility of making terms with the victor. Antony's rage, and Cleopatra's art in calming it down, combine to confirm his feeling that they can never be brought to save themselves now, and that the wisest thing to do is to go while the going is good, since they are past hope of profiting by any help or counsel that he can give them.

It is a momentous decision, and a momentous departure, for in losing Enobarbus Antony is losing his last link with that western world that he had so long served and helped to rule. All unknowing, he embarrasses Enobarbus horribly by calling for a lavish banquet on the eve of what may well be his last battle, and thanking attendant after attendant for all their faithful service, while Enobarbus and Cleopatra, the man who has finally decided to leave him and the woman whose intentions are inscrutable to the last, have to stand by and look on. It is almost more than Enobarbus can bear, and Antony rallies him and his fellows on the grief they find it impossible to conceal. Never before had Antony seemed so noble a master, and so well worth defending loyally to the end. His influence is almost that of the young king going the rounds on the eve of Agincourt,

> That the poor wretch, panting and pale before,
> Beholding him, plucks comfort from his looks.

But it is too late to turn back. Enobarbus has made up his mind to go, and Shakespeare ingeniously incorporates his going in a mysterious episode related by Plutarch, who says that the night patrols in the streets of Alexandria claimed to have heard sounds of music and the ecstatic cry of the Bacchanals passing away into the distance, as if it were Antony's luck leaving him for ever.

The remorse of Enobarbus, and his death within earshot of the Roman sentinels, constitute as strange an end as may be imagined for any Shakespearean clown, and the spectators might well be dissatisfied if they saw the play go on to its end without a moment of the kind of humour they had been led to expect from Armin, but the author has taken care to avoid that. With so long a cast list as this play has, it is evident that there was scope for any amount of part-doubling, and at the very end Shakespeare introduces a clown after the old Armin fashion, sturdy and independent, and ready to give gratuitous advice to anyone who would listen to him, even to the Queen of Egypt when making arrangements for her own death. Again and again she tries, with repeated farewells, to dismiss him and get on with the business of dying, but he will not be got rid of until he has delivered himself of everything he wants to say about asps and the inadvisability of touching or feeding them because they are poisonous and not at all suitable for keeping as pets. As last he goes, however, and leaves Cleopatra free to launch out upon her magnificent closing scene. Shakespeare has performed an incredible *tour-de-force* in this play by writing memorable death scenes for his two great lovers and, unexpectedly enough, the comic man, and giving each in turn the complete run of the stage to die in. And, as happens with certain others of his particular effects, he never did it again, but went on to something completely different.

To make a sympathetic character out of such a man as Coriolanus was a challenge indeed. Fantastically brave, strong and straightforward, he was also arrogant and disagreeable, intolerant of other people's opinions and unrestrained in his language, a public hero and, practically at the same time, a public nuisance. Plutarch makes this very clear at the outset when writing his life, so Shakespeare must have seen well enough what a task was before him when making this man's story a vehicle for Burbage. Writing for Alleyn, in the old days, it could have been done in the manner of Marlowe, making the man a kind of Roman Tamburlaine and his part a continued thunderstorm, but the story and the character were worth more than that. Coriolanus, as Plutarch describes him, was a human being with the inconsistencies of humanity, and the challenge to poet and player was to show what manner of man he was, and how what he was, for good or ill, influenced so much of what he did.

His reputation among the citizens is built up before his entrance by the First Citizen with his voluble stump-oratory and the more cautious and tolerant views of the Second Citizen who heckles him. As a result Caius Marcius gets his effect, on arrival, with very little verbal violence. His language is forceful, but there is no need for him to shout, as his bull-at-a-gate technique has already been outlined expressively by other people. It is, in effect, just what had been done with the fierce mutual passions of Antony and Cleopatra. The audience has been given such a clear impression from preliminary reports that it barely realises, if at all, that it has had little or no personal demonstration by the protagonists. Now, when he appears, his words are scornful enough, but have too many consonants in them for a bellowing technique. The insults in his speech are a matter of biting, not banging or trumpeting, and the trouble about them is that they are obviously the thoughts of a shrewd, perceptive mind, and are all the more intolerable because they ring like unpalatable truth. Contrary to the carefully-preconceived opinion, it is with Coriolanus as it was with Iago. Noisy declamation of his lines weakens instead of strengthening them because it blurs the image of the mind behind them all. Irving's Coriolanus was the last new Shakespearean part he played, and was a failure, because by that time he was physically too old for Coriolanus, while Ellen Terry was too young for Volumnia, and would have been so if she had lived to be a hundred. That grim old battleaxe of a Roman matron, whose maternal supervision had made Coriolanus what he was, had been written to be played by a young man whose day of successful female impersonation was almost over, and not for anyone whose essential womanliness was her outstanding quality.

By the time the first act comes to an end, the spectators have had a chance to get their impression of Coriolanus from a rapid review of his best qualities. He has been seen in violent action, rallying beaten soldiers and putting new heart into them by the wealth and variety of his objurgations, rushing into danger with such disregard of it that his followers first abandon him for lost and then, seeing him alive and in difficulties, renew their attack in order to fetch him out, and finally, with a word of scorn for the men who have turned aside from fighting to look for loot, riding off post-haste to support his general, Cominius, in another action a mile away, where the officers and soldiers alike applaud him. Burbage has been allowed to create his effect here by rapid physical activity, which came easily to him, instead of vocal violence, which obviously did not.

From the prose scene that opens the second act one may reasonably assume that the part of Menenius was played by Armin, who was known to be not only an actor but a common pamphleteer—what we should now call a free-lance journalist—and would know how to hold the attention of an audience when delivering such a social and political lecture as he does to the resentful tribunes. It is on a different footing from his verse fable in the first scene of all, and appeals to the reason rather than the feelings of the audience, making a convenient interlude between the visible triumphs of Marcius in the field and his sudden popularity in Rome, leading to his candidature for the consulship.

Here, unexpectedly enough, the play introduces a point of high comedy. Reference is made repeatedly to Marcius's reluctance to canvass for the votes of people he despises, and to appear before them in the 'gown of humility', the white *toga candida* from which the candidate for office takes his name. The sight of a fire-eating general soliciting their support from civilian voters, and horribly embarrassed in the process, can be humorous enough, but the visual effect, to the spectators of Shakespeare's time, had an extra spice because of associations which are now obsolete and forgotten.

Whatever the religious feelings of Englishmen as a whole, it was cheaper to go to church than to be 'presented' and fined for staying away, and the appearance of Coriolanus on the stage, in more or less Elizabethan dress with a white sheet draped over it, was very like the not unfamiliar Sunday sight of a neighbour standing before the congregation, undergoing penance in a white sheet for doing something improper. This gives his conversation with his first brace of possible voters a slightly ribald undercurrent, as it was usually part of the penitent's duty to confess his fault and explain what led him to it. That opening line, 'You know the cause, sirs, of my standing here', might well be the prelude, in another place, to an admission of drunken and disorderly conduct, brawling in the churchyard, spreading slanderous rumours about respectable parishioners, or unseemly behaviour with someone else's wife, to be followed by repentance and promises of amendment in the future. This almost comic scene lightens the tension, and in fact takes him well on the way to the consulship, until the tribunes hastily inflame the voters in the other direction, with accusations shrewdly framed to bring out the worst in him when they meet face to face. His own opinions on the importance of degrees and discipline are those of Ulysses, but they are not expressed with anything like Ulysses's tact, and actually lead to fighting in the streets. It is not merely thundrous ill-temper; there is a shrewdness and reasoning behind it all that makes him dangerous. The sense of the words is as important as the sound, and the only antidote to it is to stir up the blind, unreasoning rage of the mob and, after a nearly-successful attempt to kill him, to succeed at last in having him driven into exile, never to return on pain of death.

As with Lear on the heath and Timon in the wilderness, Coriolanus reveals that adversity brings out the best in him. His leave-taking shows a consideration for his family and friends that we have not seen before, and the cadence of his lines is full of encouragement and tenderness, so that we see the good side of Volumnia's training of him. It is she who breaks out into curses against 'all trades in Rome', and he, for a change, who urges calmness. It is the same when he arrives in Antium, and stands warming himself at Aufidius's hearth. The servants of the great house are apprehensive even while they sneer at him as a 'poor gentleman' and try to turn him away, but he stands quietly and speaks tolerantly —save for one flash of warning when a man lays an incautious hand on him—and keeps his temper as he never kept it when challenging the tribunes in Rome. It is another exercise of that authority that Burbage seems to have been able to command from those early days when he was Richard of Gloucester terrifying the halberdier, and it practically never leaves him until the last scene of all. His rebuff to Menenius is tempered with a slight concession made wholly out of kindness, and there is a ring of Richard II at his most moving in the moment when he unbends to the extent of admitting his wife's kiss. Little by little we see—and hear—him waver in his own resolution, and at the climax there is a stage-direction enforcing one of those great Shakespearean silences that are so much more eloquent than words.

The direction, 'Holds her by the hand silent', at the end of Volumnia's great final speech, is a realisation of what, according to Plutarch, actually happened. We can understand Shakespeare's appreciation of the dramatic value of this point of detail, and his anxiety to make sure that the point was not overlooked in production, and this, in combination with the nature and extent of the other stage-directions in the play, tells us something more about the circumstances of its composition. The play is being written at some distance from the theatre, and the author is by no means certain of being on hand at every rehearsal and available at all times to answer questions about how this or that scene should go. He is no longer a full-time acting member of the King's Men, but is 'William Shakespeare of Stratford upon Avon in the Countye of Warwicke gentleman of the age of xlviii yeres or thereabouts' as he was to be described in a legal document of 1612, and though he still writes plays for his old colleagues, someone else will have to do the producing, so it is incumbent on him to make his own ideas and intentions as clear as possible.

This is particularly important in the first act, where the campaigning scenes can easily degenerate into a muddle if the actors are not perfectly clear what they are doing, and why. The addition of the word 'hastily' to the normal 'enter a Messenger' in the first scene is a hint to the actors that the news he brings is unexpected and, to a good many people, alarming. The injunction to Coriolanus's wife and mother, at their first entry, to 'set them downe on two lowe stooles and sowe' establishes at once a slightly humdrum domestic scene, in which the older lady is obviously irritated with the younger one's tendency to mope. Valeria's arrival 'with an Usher, and a Gentlewoman' shows at once that she is a person of some quality, and must play her part accordingly, as one who has access to the latest war news and can retail it as having heard it from a member of the Senate. It is not mere prattle, but is meant to be heard and understood, as it explains that there are two military operations on hand, one under Cominius, against the main Volscian army in the open field, and the other, under his two subordinates, against Corioli itself. In due course we have to see both operations in turn, with quite precise instructions about the storming of Corioli on the one hand and the entry of Cominius 'as it were in retire, with soldiers' on the other, and we can understand how Caius Marcius, by enthusiasm and hard riding, contrives to be in both.

A little eight-line scene after the taking of Corioli shows Titus Lartius entering 'with a Lieutenant, other Souldiers, and a Scout', and indicates that the Lieutenant is being left in command of the captured city while Lartius himself is marching off to join Marcius and Cominius in the other action, with the Scout to show him the way. It is all very necessary, if the action is to be understood at all, for the various bodies of troops to know what they are supposed to have been doing, or what they are proposing to do when they come on the stage, and the author puts it meticulously down in the stage-directions so that somebody may be able to make sure that they *do* know, in case he is not there to tell them himself.

This principle about stage-directions is noticeable in all Shakespeare's last plays, written when he was living at Stratford and no longer in daily and day-long contact with the theatre. In *The Winter's Tale* there are hardly any, the names of the characters being listed at the opening of each scene, as in classical texts, but even here, once or twice, we may see the *Coriolanus* touch in the shape of a brief indication what they are doing there. The name of Hermione is followed once by the words 'to her trial', and once at the end by 'like a statue'—the only stage-direction in that supremely important and moving scene. These, surely, are not even instructions to the actor or the stage-manager; their appeal is to the *reader*—the actor, sharer or manager who sees the manuscript for the first time, or the Examiner of Plays who has to be assured that the argument has 'no offence in't' and will understand it the more readily for an indication that the scene he is about to read is a trial scene, or that it is laid in a place with statues in it. These few words are the forerunners of the place-indications which were introduced in the 18th century and so long hampered Shakespearean production by their suggestion of repeated changes of scenery and consequent delays.

The impatience of Leontes, and his fierce resentment of question or contradiction, would come easily to, and be readily accepted from, the Burbage who had recently played Coriolanus. Autolycus is a part in the regular Tarlton-Armin vein of rather disreputable cheerfulness combined with a talent for expressive prose, consequential or confidential as the occasion requires, and the sheep-shearing feast in the fourth act gives opportunities for dancing and song. Similar musical interludes occur in the course of *Cymbeline,* and the stage-directions suddenly break out in detail in the latter part of the play, to prevent the battle scenes from being either scamped in production or made wildly incomprehensible and confusing. Cymbeline himself is rather a thankless part through four acts of the play, with nothing worth remembering to say or do except the already-cited opening of the third act, but in the last scene he is given a chance to show the old Burbage versatility by running through a whole gamut of emotions, condemning people to death and reprieving them, losing a wife and recovering two long-lost sons, a daughter and a newly-appreciated son-in-law, and dominating the action to the very end.

A striking throw-back to earlier days is provided by *King Henry VIII,* which belongs to this last period and yet serves to round off the original cycle of the Histories after the manner of Hall's *Chronicle,* from which the general scheme of the cycle is derived. The story is taken from the *Chronicle,* with contributions from George Cavendish's life of Wolsey (unpublished, but known to have been available in manuscript), and Foxe's *Actes and Monuments of the Martyrs.* As a complete reaction from *The Winter's Tale* it purports to represent the incontrovertible facts of history, and on its original presentation at the Globe, where it was put on with such enthusiastic attention to detail that the off-stage sound-effects set the theatre on fire, it appeared under the title *All is True,* proclaiming to the public in general that it was a story founded on recorded fact.

That attitude produced two notable results in the writing of it. In the first place, Hall's narrative goes into such detail in the matter of pageantry and costume worn at the great state functions (many of which he personally saw) that it is worth transcribing his descriptions into the appropriate stage-directions, in order to create the right effect. Once again, the author who cannot count on being able to supervise all the rehearsals has to put down in some detail exactly what he wants, often supplementing it with a descriptive commentary by the spectators, which may serve to piece out the imperfections of the production.

In the same way, the nature of the piece instinctively calls for that variation of pace, and use of frequent double-endings, that had been necessary in the historical and diplomatic scenes in *Henry IV*. The new play is in some ways parallel to the old, in that its theme is the gradual development of a king. Its balance has been somewhat upset, as with *Measure for Measure,* by the abandonment of the boy actress in favour of the leading lady. As this advancement of Isabella gave increased prominence to the part of her adversary Angelo, so the emergence of Katharine as a tragedy-queen led to the aggrandisement of Wolsey, and the tendency to huddle up the last act of the play, after his fall, as a matter of little interest, just as was done with the last act of *The Merchant of Venice* when the star of the company played Shylock instead of Bassanio. It was different, however, with a male Katharine; she would fall into line, almost, with Buckingham, as a figure broken in her turn by the power and influence of Wolsey, but her tragedy would be merely incidental, a step onward in the main story, which is that of the gradual independence of Henry, and his rise to supreme power.

Quite possibly the passage of time, and the stages in the king's development, were marked by changes in his appearance. It is just the sort of thing the versatile Burbage would have enjoyed, and the play gives him good opportunity for it. In the first act he is young, grateful to the cardinal, tender to his queen, well spoken-of by his courtiers for his proclamation against the extravagant following of French fashions (a step for which the chroniclers particularly commended him) and obviously enjoying himself at the cardinal's banquet. Then he has time, during the scenes describing the fall of Buckingham, to change his dress a little, and when he appears again his lines change likewise. He is fierce and abrupt with the dukes who disturb him at his meditations, troubled in mind when he turns to the cardinals for encouragement, and ready to accept the services of Gardiner, whom Wolsey has insinuated into his household. The old merriment is gone, and he is troubled within himself and short-tempered with others, both in his closet and in the court at Blackfriars. Hall's *Chronicle* says of him at this time that 'the King, which all the twenty years past had been ruled by others, and in especial by the Cardinal of York, began now to be a ruler and a king'.

As with the politics in *Coriolanus,* Shakespeare declines to take sides, but shows us the motives, opinions and exaggerations of both. We are not told precisely whether Buckingham was or was not guilty of treason, but we are given the opinion of various representative gentlemen about the court, and shown enough of Buckingham to see that, traitor or not, he has certainly been appallingly indiscreet. So here; Queen Katharine accuses Wolsey of having stirred up the king's mind against her, Wolsey denies the charge and urges his own impartiality, and Henry himself gives an independent account of the matter, exonerating the cardinal. All these speeches and arguments are important as evidence of the various speakers' opinions. It is by consideration of that evidence that the audience must make up its own mind, and so we find the evidence presented in that emphatic, judicial form, with plenty of disyllabic endings,. that has appeared in the Henry IV plays.

It is a form suggestive of grave consideration, and it usually accompanies a speech taken in whole or in part from one of the nearly-contemporary chronicles, and therefore important enough to be given every opportunity to sink into the hearer's mind. At the end of the scene, when all the arguments have been put forward and the king is ready for a definitive verdict, he meets instead with frustration and disappointment. Katharine has just put up such a good case for herself that he has been spurred into admiration of her, to the point of crying out in ringing, romantic lines,

> Prove but our marriage lawful, by my life
> And kingly dignity, we are contented
> To wear our mortal state to come with her,
> Katharine our queen, before the primest creature
> That's paragon'd o' the world.

For the moment, at least, we may believe he means it, and it is with a sense of anticlimax and frustration that we hear Campeius pronounce that the matter must be referred back, in view of the queen's absence, to some future day. The session is at an end, and has accomplished nothing.

The scene that follows, between Queen Katharine and the cardinal-legates, contains one of the best-authenticated pieces of dialogue in the play. Up to the point where she laments that her best advisers are at home in Spain, it is straight out of Hall, and Hall says he translated it from the account by Campeius's secretary, who was actually there. The continuance, with Katharine's denunciation of the legates, is Shakespeare's own contribution, because at that point the three of them went into an inner room where their attendants could not hear them. Still, the dialogue continues to be that of serious argument and judgement, not smooth-running conversation, and here, as so often elsewhere in the play, the double endings give it weight.

The next conversation between Wolsey and the king is, by contrast, smooth and conversational. Henry's lines have a double meaning, clear to the audience and to the noblemen who are in his confidence, but not to the cardinal, who has no idea that he has sent some very intimate personal memoranda to the king in the place of official papers. Double endings are few and insignificant until the king takes his abrupt and angry departure. After that, they return and continue to the end of the act. Wolsey's own soliloquies, and the accusations levelled against him by the dukes of Norfolk and Suffolk, are all deliberate pronouncements, even when uttered in the flash of anger, and it is that same deliberation that the metre fixes in the mind. Other playwrights took it up and used it more freely and indiscriminately to lay emphasis on their own verse as such, but Shakespeare employs it systematically in matters of deliberation and historical fact, and in pronouncements like those of the queen's death-scene, where all the speakers weigh their words carefully—except one, who is abruptly taken to task for it, and departs unforgiven—and are increasingly conscious of the presence of approaching death.

The scene of Wolsey's soliloquy, and the whole act that follows, keep Henry off the stage for the final transformation in the tiring-house. When he reappears, he is the Henry of Holbein, and of the crude woodcut in the 1577 edition of Holinshed—and, in 1613, the Henry of old men's memories. Moreover, he is a Henry without Wolsey, and without the need of Wolsey. He is now indeed 'a ruler and a king', quiet and conversational, with a sinister undercurrent, when he sends for Cranmer by night, and suddenly terrible when he appears to defend him at the council-board. Gardiner's attempt to be another Wolsey is snuffed like a candle, a tentative 'May it please your Grace—' is cut short by a thundrous, 'No, sir, it does not please me!', and in the speech that follows, the double endings come down like hammer-strokes. Substitute equivalents of one syllable, and the speech is unimaginably weakened; read it beside one of Holbein's later portraits of the king, and it falls into place as the natural accompaniment of that set mouth and slight but terrifying frown. (Plate IV.)

A ballad about the burning of the Globe in 1613 mentions 'Burbidge' and 'the Foole', and we may justly assume that both Burbage and Armin were in the original cast. Downes, in the late 17th century, said that Lowin was instructed in the king's part by Shakespeare himself, but he said the same thing about Taylor's Hamlet, and Shakespeare had been dead for some years before Taylor joined the company at all, so we can hardly take Downes as an absolutely irrefutable authority. Lowin may have played the part later on, but it seems clear, on detailed examination, that it was cut to Burbage's training and experience, which Shakespeare knew as well as anyone.

As for 'the Foole', we may wonder whether Armin did not perhaps play the lively and outspoken Old Lady, who has such a frank, uncompromising view of Anne Boleyn's prospects, and such promptitude in making something for herself out of the birth of an heir to the Throne. Be that as it may, what seems more than likely is that he was the Porter in the last scene but one. Once more we may remember that mention of Tarlton's face looking through the curtains, and it may well be that Tarlton's pupil and successor could produce the same result when, whatever he had done earlier, he appeared more or less *in propria persona* at the end of the play. That being so, his opening adjuration 'You'll leave your noise anon, ye rascals' would have a double significance for the applauding crowd that had hailed his entry—or would have done, had the play got as far as that before the conflagration put an end to an association of playwright, player, and playhouse that had lasted for 20 years. There was a new Globe in a surprisingly short time; Jonson, Fletcher and Massinger lived on, and the stars of Dryden and Betterton would soon rise to show plays and acting of a different kind to playgoers of a different generation, but the great days of the Elizabethan theatre came to an end with the passing, in the short space of six years, of two men and a building. The Globe was burned in 1613, Shakespeare died in 1616, Burbage in 1619, and the true sound of Shakespeare's lines, as he had conceived them, Burbage had interpreted them, and the boards of the Globe had echoed them, was silenced for ever.

APPENDIX

Text of the poem appended to the portrait of Richard Tarlton in MS. Harl. 3885, Fol. 19, in the British Library, transcribed in modern spelling.

The picture here set down
Within this letter T,
Aright doth shew the form and shape
Of Tharlton unto thee.

When he in pleasant wise
The Counterfeit exprest
Of Clown with coat of russet hue
And startups with the rest.

Who merry many made
When he appeared in sight.
The grave and wise as well as rude
At him did take delight.

The party now is gone
And closely clad in clay,
Of all the Jesters in the land
He bare the praise away.

Now hath he played his part
And sure he is of this,
If he in Christ did die, to live
With him in lasting bliss.

*See plate 3

INDEX